Learning to Love

The Politics of Marriage and Gender:
Global Issues in Local Contexts

Series Editor: Péter Berta

The Politics of Marriage and Gender: Global Issues in Local Contexts series from Rutgers University Press fills a gap in research by examining the politics of marriage and related practices, ideologies, and interpretations, and addresses the key question of how the politics of marriage has affected social, cultural, and political processes, relations, and boundaries. The series looks at the complex relationships between the politics of marriage and gender, ethnic, national, religious, racial, and class identities, and analyzes how these relationships contribute to the development and management of social and political differences, inequalities, and conflicts.

Joanne Payton, *Honor and the Political Economy of Marriage: Violence against Women in the Kurdistan Region of Iraq*

Rama Srinivasan, *Courting Desire: Litigating for Love in North India*

Hui Liu, Corinne Reczek, and Lindsey Wilkinson, eds., *Marriage and Health: The Well-Being of Same-Sex Couples*

Sara Smith, *Intimate Geopolitics: Love, Territory, and the Future on India's Northern Threshold*

Rebecca Joubin, *Mediating the Uprising: Narratives of Gender and Marriage in Syrian Television Drama*

Raksha Pande, *Learning to Love: Arranged Marriages and the British Indian Diaspora*

Learning to Love

Arranged Marriages and the British Indian Diaspora

RAKSHA PANDE

RUTGERS UNIVERSITY PRESS

NEW BRUNSWICK, CAMDEN, AND NEWARK, NEW JERSEY, AND LONDON

Library of Congress Cataloging-in-Publication Data
Names: Pande, Raksha, author.
Title: Learning to love: arranged marriages and the
British Indian diaspora / Raksha Pande.
Description: New Brunswick, New Jersey: Rutgers University Press, [2021] |
Series: The politics of marriage and gender: global issues in local contexts |
Includes bibliographical references and index.
Identifiers: LCCN 2020027648 | ISBN 9780813599632 (paperback) |
ISBN 9780813599649 (hardcover) | ISBN 9780813599656 (epub) |
ISBN 9780813599663 (mobi) | ISBN 9780813599670 (pdf)
Subjects: LCSH: Arranged marriage—Great Britain. | East Indians—
Marriage customs and rites—Great Britain.
Classification: LCC HQ802 .P36 2021 | DDC 392.50941—dc23
LC record available at https://lccn.loc.gov/2020027648

A British Cataloging-in-Publication record for this book is available
from the British Library.

♾ The paper used in this publication meets the requirements of the American
National Standard for Information Sciences—Permanence of Paper for Printed
Library Materials, ANSI Z39.48-1992.

www.rutgersuniversitypress.org

Manufactured in the United States of America

For my parents and their *Pande*monium

CONTENTS

Series Foreword
  BY PÉTER BERTA   ix
Preface and
  Acknowledgments   xiii

1 The Politics of Marriage and Migration in
    Postcolonial Britain   1

2 Becoming Modern and British: Enacting Citizenship
    through Arranged Marriages   21

3 Continuing Traditions as a Matter of Arrangement   42

4 Becoming a "Suitable Boy" and a "Good Girl"   59

5 Learning to Love   77

6 The Ties That Bind: Marriage, Belonging, and Identity   96

7 Conclusion   112

References   119
Index   131

SERIES FOREWORD

The politics of marriage (and divorce) is an often-used strategic tool in various social, cultural, economic, and political identity projects as well as in symbolic conflicts between ethnic, national, or religious communities. Despite having multiple strategic applicabilities, pervasiveness in everyday life, and huge significance in performing and managing identities, the politics of marriage is surprisingly underrepresented in both the international book publishing market and the social sciences.

The Politics of Marriage and Gender: Global Issues in Local Contexts is a series from Rutgers University Press examining the politics of marriage as a phenomenon embedded into and intensely interacting with much broader social, cultural, economic, and political processes and practices such as globalization; transnationalization; international migration; human trafficking; vertical social mobility; the creation of symbolic boundaries between ethnic populations, nations, religious denominations, or classes; family formation; and struggles for women's and children's rights. The series primarily aims to analyze practices, ideologies, and interpretations related to the politics of marriage and to outline the dynamics and diversity of relatedness—interplay and interdependence, for instance—between the politics of marriage and the broader processes and practices mentioned above. In other words, most books in the series devote special attention to how the politics of marriage and these processes and practices mutually shape and explain each other.

The series concentrates on, among other things, the complex relationships between the politics of marriage and gender, ethnic, national, religious, racial, and class identities globally and examines how these relationships contribute to the development and management of social, cultural, and political differences, inequalities, and conflicts.

The series seeks to publish single-authored books and edited volumes that develop a gap-filling and thought-provoking critical perspective, that are well-balanced between a high degree of theoretical sophistication and empirical richness, and that cross or rethink disciplinary, methodological, or theoretical boundaries. The thematic scope of the series is intentionally left broad to encourage creative submissions that fit within the perspectives outlined above.

Among the potential topics closely connected with the problem sensitivity of the series are "honor"-based violence; arranged (forced, child, etc.) marriage; transnational marriage markets, migration, and brokerage; intersections of marriage and religion/class/race; the politics of agency and power within marriage; reconfiguration of family: same-sex marriage/union; the politics of love, intimacy, and desire; marriage and multicultural families; the (religious, legal, etc.) politics of divorce; the causes, forms, and consequences of polygamy in contemporary societies; sport marriage; refusing marriage; and so forth.

Learning to Love: Arranged Marriages and the British Indian Diaspora is a nuanced and thought-provoking analysis of the social and cultural dynamics of arranged marriage practices among the British Indian diaspora living in northern England. Drawing on five years of ethnographic research, Raksha Pande convincingly shows that arranged marriages are neither homogenous nor timeless phenomena but increasingly varied and flexible sociocultural practices that are reshaped and reinterpreted by each British Indian family to suit individual or family-level ambitions, aspirations, and identities. Investigating the contemporary lived experience of arranged marriage, *Learning to Love* also demonstrates in a fascinating way why arranged marriages are inextricably connected to negotiating citizenship and (trans)national belonging and how arranged marriage practices have been continuously transformed in order to contribute to the creation of a prized narrative of collective identity, which portrays the British Indian diaspora as "modern and progressive migrants." In this illuminating book, Pande not only illustrates how love and romance may play an important role in partner selection, but also brilliantly highlights the patterns and dynamics of interpersonal and affective negotiations concerning marriage—with a special focus on intergenerational cooperation and conflict management.

Péter Berta

University College London

School of Slavonic and East European Studies

PREFACE AND
ACKNOWLEDGMENTS

This book presents an intergenerational ethnographic study of arranged marriages as they are practiced among the British Indian diaspora. The research featured in this book examines the challenges of understanding marriage-related migration. It illuminates the shifting multicultural realties of our world by analyzing the politics of intimacy evident in the intertwining of marriage and migration, the gender relations and affective registers in arranged marriages, and the issues of identity and belonging that have shaped arranged marriage practices in Britain.

I begin by introducing the academic and policy debates on marriage and migration in Britain. I discuss the problem of defining arranged marriage practices by first concentrating on the politics of intimacy that accompanies marriage-related migration and second by critiquing the dualism-driven vocabulary of scholars and policy makers that sets up arranged marriages as the "other" to Western marriages and Western modernity at large. I will further a postcolonial approach to arranged marriages by rethinking the practice of arranged marriage through a fluid epistemological dynamic of negotiation, translation, and hybridity in contrast to a more fixed ontological matrix of essentialism and origin. Chapter 2 unpacks the different ways in which arranged marriages are defined by British Indians. It highlights that the term "arranged marriage" covers a spectrum of practices. Everyone interviewed during my research referred to arranged marriages in its different forms such as a mode of matchmaking, semi-arranged marriages, love-cum-arranged marriages, and arranged weddings. This chapter presents an examination of these views by conducting a deconstructive analysis of the terms "arrangement" and "choice." It argues that there is no single definition of arranged marriages, but a varied understanding of the terms "arrangement" and "choice" results in the various ways the practice of arranged marriage plays out in the lives of its practitioners. The conflation between the terms "arranged marriage" and "forced marriage" is also analyzed. Chapter 3 provides an account of the different processes involved in arranging marriages. It sets out in detail the various methods, tactics, and deliberations involved in arranging a marriage. It discusses the role of choice, instinct, compromise, and negotiations involved in arranging a match and describes how the decision to have an arranged marriage is made with the aid of informal channels such as family networks and more recently formal channels such as matrimony websites and professional matchmakers. It argues that for my participants the delicate orchestration of the matchmaking process plays an important role in the sustenance of an Indian identity but also modifications to the process (such as the use of websites and chaperoned dates) further the narrative of a modern and *British* Indian aspect of their identities. Chapter 4 focuses on the gender relations and gender politics that underscore the finding of a spouse through arranged marriage practices. It discusses the criteria employed in matchmaking such as the endogamous preferences of religion, caste, and class. More significantly it shows that among my participants the burden of expectations, albeit different, was present for both men and women. While for women the stress was on personal appearance and the notion of "reputation as a good girl," the men were subject to pressures of being "a suitable boy with a steady well-paying job." This chapter shows that although traditional gender roles were promoted as part of the matchmaking process, there were also many ways in which young men and women subverted them to tailor the arranged marriage practice to suit their personal notion of an ideal partner. Chapter 5 focuses on the love stories of people who found their partner through an arranged marriage. It discusses the various ways in which the concept of love is understood and experienced by British Indians of different generations. It theorizes the experience of love as a social construct by highlighting the various idioms of love used by British Indians, such as in the conceptualizations of "love as a form of learning," to reveal the affective register of arranged marriage practices. It also makes a case for an epistemology of love by providing a genealogical exploration of how love has come to be understood within contemporary Western society. The final chapter analyzes the motivations that drive the exercise of arranged marriages. I explore the different reasons that my respondents gave for having an arranged marriage for themselves and/or for their children. The focus is on exploring how a migrant subjectivity that straddles multiple senses of being and belonging was central to the justifications put forward for continuing the practice of arranged marriages in Britain.

This book would not have been possible without the generosity of the people who took part in the research. I thank them for inviting me into their homes and sharing their stories with me. Many of the ideas featured in the book were germinated during my doctoral studies with Anoop Nayak and Peter Phillimore. They were excellent thesis supervisors who encouraged me to think critically and ethically and to also have confidence in my abilities—for this I will be forever indebted to them. Péter Berta invited me to participate in this books series, and I thank him for his patience and advice. Thanks to Kimberly Guinta and Jasper Chang at Rutgers University Press for providing excellent editorial guidance.

Chapter I contains some ideas previously featured in *Geography Compass* 2014, 8(2), 75–86 (Wiley-Blackwell, Oxford), and a version of chapter 2 was previously published in *Social and Cultural Geography* 2016, 17(3), 380–400 (Taylor and Francis, London). I am grateful to these publishers for granting me the permission to draw upon this material. Thanks to Nusra Latif Qureshi for permission to use her artwork *Familiar Desires II* as the cover image for this book.

I am also grateful for the supportive and inspiring environment at the Newcastle University's School of Geography, Politics and Sociology, where I would like to thank my colleagues, in particular Ali Copeland, Nick Megoran, Alison Stenning, Jon Pugh, and Simon Tate. The friendship of Jane Carnaffan has been a pillar of strength for me throughout the writing of this book and beyond and for which I am eternally thankful. Lastly, I would like to thank Patrice Carbonneau—tu me montres le sens de l'amour chaque jour.

Raksha Pande
Newcastle, September 2019

Learning to Love

1

The Politics of Marriage and Migration in Postcolonial Britain

Marriage is a running joke; if it's a good joke, it's a good marriage.

–Martin Amis, interview, "On the Same Page"

Marriage is a bundle of rights.

–Edmund Leach, *Rethinking Anthropology*

This book is about the two most abiding concerns of human life—love and marriage—and their pursuit among British Indians. While the search for love and finding a life partner are universal concerns, the ways in which people go about realizing them vary considerably all around the world. For most people in the Western world, companionate love marriages, where the search for a marriage partner is left to the caprices of romantic love and individual choice and may or may not result in a long-term union, are the norm. However, this is not the case everywhere; in many non-Western societies, marriages are regarded as a matter of family rather than individual choice and romantic love is seen as an outcome rather than a condition for marriage. The practice commonly referred to as arranged marriage is common in South Asia, the Middle East, and large parts of Africa. Migrant communities in the West that trace their origin to these regions also practice it. Indeed, arranged marriages occupy an awkward place in contemporary Western cultures as they are often seen as anachronistic to the demands of (post)modern liberal societies. Stereotypical representations of arranged marriages in the media (Alibhai-Brown 2019) routinely conflate them with forced marriages and depict them as less than, and certainly other to, mainstream marriage norms (Penn 2011). Its practitioners are seen as victims of their illiberal cultures (Walker and Jolly 2019), and social policy reports find them as barriers to social cohesion and integration (Casey 2016). Within the immigration policy arena, arranged marriage practices are held up to scrutiny because they are regarded as strategies that increase immigration and more recently in Europe (with a growing right-wing climate) as posing a challenge to the integration of migrant populations in host societies. In the United Kingdom, migration policy has a long history of regarding arranged marriage practices as counter to Britishness. As early as 1976, the first report from the Select Committee on Race Relations and Immigration quotes a foreign and commonwealth office minister as saying, "We would want to discourage the arranged marriage system. [We hope] that more and more parents will respect the rights of their children" (cited in Jhutti 1998, 59). The now abolished (by the Labour government in 1997) notorious primary purpose rule required foreign nationals married to British citizens to prove that the primary purpose of their marriage was not to obtain British residency. It disproportionately targeted British citizens wanting to marry someone from the Indian subcontinent as their practice of arranged marriages was not seen as the basis of a normal British marital relationship (Hall 2002). This pathologization of arranged marriage practices is also evident in more recent policy discourses. In her analysis of the 2001 British governmental white paper "Secure Borders, Safe Haven: Integration with Diversity in Modern Britain," which set out the terms for the 2002 Immigration and Asylum Act, Irene Gedalof (2007, 84) comments, "The focus of new proposals to tighten controls on marrying British nationals as a way of gaining citizenship is clearly on 'those communities that continue the practice of arranged marriages' (2001, 18), thus producing Britain's Asian communities as a particular problem to be managed." This management of the Asian "problem" of arranged marriage can also be seen in successive immigration policy reforms in 2012, when the new Coalition government raised the minimum income threshold required for a British citizen to bring a spouse or other family member to the United Kingdom from outside the European Union to £25,600, with additional income required for children. The government also increased the probationary spousal leave to remain from two to five years.

While these policy changes have been presented as measures that "protect the taxpayer" and the welfare state, they have also been increasingly linked to questions of belonging and citizenship. As Byrne (2015) notes, the construction of the good citizen in Britain has been racialized

and gendered through a series of immigration acts that enshrine normative assumptions about the superiority of white Western forms of marriage over others. D'Aoust (2013, 2018) has shown that marriage migration
management practices within Britain have led to the increasing "securi-
tization of marriage" (2018, 43), where arranged marriages are subject to
"everyday bordering" practices (Yuval-Davis, Wemyss, and Cassidy 2018)
by being seen as suspicious from the start. She argues that when "the historically and geographically specific (but universalized) notion of the romanti-
cally bonded couple as the base unit of society" has been mobilized as the
central basis of marriage migration policy, couples such as those practicing
arranged marriages then always "stand out" as anomalies (D'Aoust 2018, 42).
This biopolitical governmentality of marriage migration means that the
trope of the romantic bonded (mostly heterosexual) couple, as the basis of
society, also feeds into the implicit assumptions of a racialized "good"
citizen—one whose rights should be protected and whose transnational
marriage should be seen as genuine. Consequently, in a migration policy scenario where a politics of intimacy marks arranged marriage practices as suspect, a stratification of citizens' rights (based on their marriage preferences)
has taken place (D'Aoust 2018). More widely, in mainland Europe too, governments and policy makers see arranged marriage practices as posing a
challenge to the very norms on which the discourses of European national
identities are based. For example, as Myrdahl (2010) has argued in the case of
Norwegian family reunification legislation, romantic love is employed as the
basis of constructing the idea of national subjects by citing its existence as a
test to determine the legitimacy of a marriage union. She has interpreted
Norwegian immigration legislation as a process of advancing a "racialised
project of national belonging" by putting the marital practices and preferences of some of its citizens from minority ethnic groups under scrutiny.
Similar arguments have been made about marriage legislation in Denmark
(Schmidt 2011) and the Netherlands (Bonjour and de Hart 2013), where
arranged marriages are seen as being counter to "Danishness" and Dutch
identity, respectively.

I would contend that family reunion and immigration legislation play
politics with migrant rights and citizenship to advance domestic national-
istic agendas. For instance, in Britain, as Ahmad (2006, 273) has argued,
"The trope of arranged marriages is used to circulate as a sign of [British

Asian] 'otherness' and as a site for intervention and domestication of that otherness." People who have arranged marriages are viewed as bearers of cultures that are in contrast to and pose a threat to the mainstream. Moreover, resistance to arranged marriages can become a convenient tool for governments to tighten legislation to shore up national boundaries. This politics of marriage migration elides arranged marriages with forced marriages and consequently leaves little space for acknowledging the complexity, diversity, and flexibility of factors and motivations that go into the making of an arranged marriage.

The politics of marriage typically assumes a singular definition of arranged marriages—a contract between families where individual choice and agency have no role in matchmaking. In this book I argue that this is a simplistic and incomplete picture of the practice of arranged marriage as it operates among British Indians. I show that arranged marriages are an increasingly flexible and dynamic matchmaking practice that involves, among others, considerations of the choice and preference of the individuals getting married. I analyze the various discourses, performances, and motivations that underscore the finding of a partner through an arranged marriage. I provide a postcolonial rethinking of the category of arranged marriage by highlighting the affective engagements and reflexive understandings of the practice. The focus of my research is on people who have chosen to have an arranged marriage. This is an important distinction to make—this is not a book about forced marriages, although many people assume that forced and arranged marriages are the same. As I illustrate, the term "arranged marriage" covers a spectrum of practices, with forced marriages on one extreme. My concern is with researching the popularity of this phenomenon among the Indian diaspora in Britain for whom arranged marriages remain the norm. I elicit the voices of differently placed family members about what arranged marriage means to them and more importantly discuss the value of this practice in their social biographies, which straddle multiple places and multiple senses of belonging. The questions of choice and agency are also addressed, but with reference to how arranged marriage norms are subverted and modified (rather than a rejection of the practice per se) with each new generation remaking the tradition to suit their diasporic identities. This becomes even more significant when seeking to understand the continuation of this tradition among second- and third-generation British Indians, for whom such motivations as obligations to kinship networks from the old country may not always be so binding. In sum, the book asks and answers three simple but significant questions about arranged marriage practices: How do British Indians define arranged marriages? What are the different ways in which these marriages are arranged? And what is the significance of this practice in the lives of the British Indian diaspora?

Through a theorization of the contemporary lived experience of arranged marriage, I argue for a new approach to understanding this practice and conceptualize it as a discursive practice as opposed to a timeless traditional custom. I show that, far from being a homogeneous tradition, arranged marriages involve a variety of different matchmaking practices where each family makes its own version of British Indian arranged marriages to suit modern identities and ambitions. These arranged marriages are inspired by memories of Indian traditions and family customs, experiences of British-style Western marriages, and representations of the nonresident Indian (NRI) wedding in Bollywood films. One of the main contributions of this book is to deconstruct the term "arranged marriage" and highlight the elastic nature of the practice. Arranged marriage can mean different things to different people, which in the context of British Indians is a very large umbrella. A grandmother, a mother, and a granddaughter all might have had what can be described as an arranged marriage, but they all would have had very different understandings and experiences of the practice. As I show in this book, the term "arranged marriage" covers a spectrum of practices. There is no singular definition, but a varied understanding of the terms "arrangement" and "choice" results in its many distinct and interrelated forms. Indian migrant families in Britain skillfully adopt and actively negotiate traditional arranged marriage cultural norms to tailor arranged marriage practices to different types such as semi-arranged marriage, love-cum-arranged marriage, and arranged wedding to define their own unique way of doing arranged marriages in Britain (as detailed in chapter 2). They justify their changes and the different degree of allowances made for the role of romantic love and individual choice as key strategies though which they not only embrace Western modernity but also enact their own version of a British Indian citizenship. I also show that contrary to popular conceptions of arranged marriage as a cold and calculated practice, considerations of love and romance form an important part of arranged marriages. Its practitioners distinguish between different forms of love and the accompanying obligations to individuals, family, and society at large. Although it is not regarded as the sole basis of marriage, romantic love is nonetheless seen as a key ingredient in sustaining a marital union. This book illustrates the grammar of love used by British Indians, such as in the conceptualizations of "love as a form of learning," to reveal the affective register of arranged marriage practices.

Although the empirical focus of the book is the British Indian diaspora, the conclusions have relevance in illuminating the social, (ethno)political, and economic significance of arranged marriages more widely. The question of how and in what ways minority ethnic populations integrate into mainstream society has moved to center stage in debates on migration and multiculturalism, not just in Britain but also in other migrant-receiving countries in Europe, North America, and Australia. In the current political climate of Brexit and the muscular nationalism of Trump's America, exemplified in increasing hostility toward immigrants and their cultural practices, it is even more important that we make an attempt to understand cultural practices such as arranged marriages beyond easy generalizations and stereotypes.

The Problem of Defining Arranged Marriages

It is important to make clear at the outset the difference between arranged and forced marriage. In arranged marriages the arrangement involves matchmaking by parents and family but is not forced. The option to decline the proposed spouse is always present. For me, arranged marriages can be better defined as a mode of matchmaking in which "a cultural logic of desire" (Del Rosario 2005, 253) is administered and mediated by the self and the family and where the exercise of choice and agency may be conditioned by a number of socioeconomic factors. However, there is some confusion in the literature with regard to what an arranged marriage entails and its relation to other non-Western modes of matchmaking. Anthropologists have used terms such as "endogamous marriage" (marriage within the same ethnic or social groups) or "consanguineous marriage" (marriage among blood relatives, common among some Muslim populations) to contrast arranged marriages with Western-style companionate marriages. Some researchers

(Charsley and Shaw 2006; Gardner 2006; Charsley 2012) prefer the term "transnational marriages" when referring to marriages arranged between partners living in different countries. (In the case of South Asians in Britain, this refers to marriages arranged between British-born Pakistanis, Bangladeshis, or Indians with individuals resident in the Indian subcontinent.) While the term "transnational marriage" is useful in drawing attention to the ways in which migrants maintain their attachments to countries and cultures through marriage, it is important to remind ourselves that not all arranged marriages are transnational. In fact, the majority are arranged among people resident in Britain (Home Office 2001). Thus, it is important to make the trite but very often overlooked point that there is no such thing as arranged marriage singular but arranged marriages. A large variety of matchmaking and marriage practices are bunched together under this heading; so, for example, marriages contracted via the phenomenon of "mail-order brides" in Southeast Asia and Eastern Europe to people meeting their future spouse through a date or meeting suggested by their parents or relatives can be defined to some extent as arranged marriages. The only uniting factor is some element of arrangement and that they are practiced by minority populations in the West, but there is a world of difference between a "mail-order" marriage and an arranged marriage as practiced by British Indians. Moreover, British Indian arranged marriages do not lend themselves to easy generalizations, not least because they span a range of practitioners who vary considerably in their religion, caste, and class compositions, but also because much like any other social and cultural practice they are being continuously evolved, adapted, and changed to fit with their practitioners' lives. This book captures some of the complexity of the evolution of arranged marriage practices with reference to the spectrum of practices that fall under the banner of British Indian arranged marriages.

Moreover, I believe that a preoccupation (among both scholars and policy makers) with the arrangement aspect of South Asians forms of matchmaking has left unexamined the scope of affective, interpersonal, and subjective aspects of arranged marriages. The journey of life that takes a new turn when people agree to become partners through the institution of marriage, which involves, I argue, a migration of ideas, cultures, and individuals, has in the context of British Indians been reduced to notions such as forced marriage and/or immigration issues. There seems to be a commonsense understanding of the lack of love in arranged marriages and the lack of arrangement in love marriages among policy makers. The problem stems from the binary opposition of "arrangement" and "love," where both are seen as diametrically opposed to each other and on a wider scale as typifying the difference between the traditional Eastern and the modern Western cultures. It is also worth noting that there is an image of what Puar (1995, 24) calls the universal arranged marriage, which dominates media representations of this practice where arranged marriages are regarded as the other to Western marriages and an obvious contradiction is believed to exist between the South Asian and Western views of marriage. I argue that there are at least three reasons for this supposed contradiction. First, an ethnocentric public discourse in the West constructs arranged marriage as forced and projects its practitioners as having no say in whom they marry and as having given up the ideals of agency, choice, and love as prized ingredients of modern life. Second, some Western viewers exhibit a shortsightedness in regarding the development of the basis of marriage based on romantic love as a timeless norm and not as an evolving product of a particular path taken by the West in its economic and social development. And finally, many believe that the ideas of romance and desire are not compatible with arranged marriage. In the context of Indians in Britain, due to their presumed difference from the mainstream population and their construction as cultural others, many assume that it is merely arrangement that characterizes their marital practices and that they have abandoned the pursuit of romantic love and aspirations. Some research suggests that in practice love and arrangement appear as a continuum in the making of a so-called arranged marriage (Shaw and Charsley 2006; Twamley 2014), and my findings also build on this scholarship.

Researching Arranged Marriages:
A Postcolonial Approach

As an Indian who has lived in Britain for the past twelve years, my relationship with the country has been marked equally by senses of both strangeness and familiarity. While growing up in a "hill station" in India, the Britain I imagined was characterized by my love of English literature—a land of William Wordsworth's daffodils, Charlotte Brontë's moors, and Jane

Austen's heroines. Incredible though it seems to me now, I never felt the need to question this unproblematic romantic imagination in favor of a more realistic image of Britain. Also, I wasn't part of the *Midnight's Children* (Rushdie 1980) generation; I was an eighties child growing up in an India where the Raj was a distant memory and where I chose sides in cricket matches based not on national allegiances but on the relative good looks of the players.[1] So if ambivalence was the watchword of postcolonial theory, I had it in plenty. The world was becoming a more globalized place, as the media portrayed it, and all of us had a part to play in this.

It was with this frame of mind that I landed in Newcastle to pursue my doctoral research. Needless to say what I experienced was a very different Britain, and more importantly it was the first time that I learned that familiarity with a country's literature does not equip one to deal with cultural difference. I began to see that I could not remain ambivalent about my postcolonial condition when everyone I encountered engaged with me not as just a student but as an Indian, a person of color, an Asian, an immigrant, and a Third World woman. And it was at this time that I was introduced to postcolonial theory, first in English literature and later in human geography. I reread Brontë through Spivak (1985) and was encouraged to ask why a poem on daffodils was part of the Indian national curriculum when the flowers that my dad grew in our garden were marigolds. In short, this was my introduction to a new way of looking at the world around me and to notice the impact of "the critical aftermath of colonialism—cultures, discourses and critiques that lie beyond, but remain closely influenced by colonialism" (Blunt and McEwan 2002, 3).

I share this personal reflection to provide the reader with a sense of how the development of my intellectual trajectory has been instrumental in the choice of my research topic and more significantly the way I have chosen to interpret the data that form the basis of this book. Through insights derived from the rich scholarship in postcolonial theory, I have been encouraged to reexamine the question of cultural representation as in re-presentation or interpretation of a culture's practices and as in

---

1. This is a reference to the infamous "cricket test" coined by the British conservative politician Norman Tebbit when he suggested in April 1990 that immigrants and their children could not show loyalty to Britain until they supported the English cricket team.

representation or speaking on behalf of a culture (Spivak 1988; Bonnett 1993). Bonnett (1993, 13) argues that both forms of representation are linked because in order to speak for a culture we need to have found some meaning within it; that is, interpretation is always involved in representation. This book is an account of my interpretation of the cultural dynamics of the practice of arranged marriage among a people with whom I am perceived to share some facets of my ethnicity and as such for whom I am seen to be speaking. More importantly, I have asked myself whose story I am trying to narrate in this book and who is the "subject" of my research. Foucault (1972, 1999) talked about the "death of the subject" by using the term "subject" to refer to objects of ideology. He theorized without reference to the individual but concentrated on the workings of the discourses that go into the making of particular kinds of subjectivities. This sentiment has been pivotal to my research as it has allowed me to not get fixated on the subject but to appreciate the moments and processes that are produced as a result of cultural encounters. So it is not merely British Indian subjects that I have researched but the various discourses of arranged marriage (both within and outside the British Indian community) that contribute to the making of a particular kind of Indian subjectivity in Britain. In so doing, I have been partial to postcolonial and more generally poststructuralist frameworks of thought because they equip me with a vocabulary that functions beyond originary and fixed subjectivities to articulate the complex processes that are involved in the negotiation of cultural difference. The objective of postcolonial theory, as Arif Dirlik (1994, 329) suggests, is "to reveal societies globally in their complex heterogeneity and contingency." And this is what I do by bringing out the nuances of arranged marriage as practiced among a section of British society. He describes three uses of the term "postcolonial":

(a) as a literal description of conditions in formerly colonial societies, in which case the term has concrete referents, as in postcolonial societies or postcolonial intellectuals;

(b) as a description of a global condition after the period of colonialism, in which case the usage is somewhat more abstract and less concrete in reference, comparable in its vagueness to the earlier term Third World, for which it is intended as a substitute; and

(c) as a description of a discourse on the above-named conditions that is informed by the epistemological and psychic orientations that are products of those conditions. (Dirlik 1994, 332)

In the context of this research, all three goals are relevant. First, the subjects of this research are members of postcolonial societies. Migration to Britain from India would not have taken place on the scale that it did if it was not for the colonial connection between the two regions. So this book is an attempt at describing the conditions and motivations for cultural production among a people whose diasporic condition is tied with their communities' experience of colonialism. Second, the transnational connections of British Indians with their counterparts around the world also produce and establish newer modes of being in the formerly imperial society of Britain. This indicates a global condition of affairs after the effects of colonialism where the word "postcolonial societies" applies as much to postcolonial Britain as to postcolonial India. Consequently, by examining the practice of arranged marriage, I bring out the strategies, practices, and performances of identity that British Indians employ to confront and negotiate cultural difference in *postcolonial* Britain. Third and more significantly, postcolonial theory helps me to make a case for understanding "arranged marriage" as a discursive phenomenon—as a discourse reflecting the views of the Indian section of British society on matchmaking and kinship. A fundamental aspect of postcolonialism is to deconstruct the experiences of speaking and writing by which dominant discourses come into being and to understand the spatiality of power and knowledge. In a similar vein, my aim is to destabilize these dominant discourses of the "universal arranged marriage" (Puar 1995, 24) that project it merely as a characteristic of patriarchal and "undeveloped" societies. By concentrating on British Indians' own discourses of arranged marriages, I capture their own voices to highlight the diversity of arranged marriage practices by examining the subtle nuances that go into making a match. By doing this I engage in problematizing what Spivak (1990) calls the process of the West "worlding," or discursively setting apart certain parts of the world from others because of assumptions and prejudices guided by an ethnocentric view of the non-Western world. The "worlding" of the discourse of arranged marriage has been overshadowed by pejorative stereotypes and assumptions about this practice. By reconceptualizing the practice beyond its stereotypes, I provide an intimate picture of arranged marriage and its significance in the lives of British Indians.

Moreover, in order to describe how British Indians choose to practice arranged marriage in its varying forms, I find a postcolonial theoretical framework helps me to rethink the practice of arranged marriage through a fluid epistemological dynamic of negotiation, translation, and hybridity in contrast to a more fixed ontological matrix of essentialism and origin. The practice of arranged marriage is employed not only to further their ties of kinship but also to construct their identity narratives as British Indians. The decision to have an arranged marriage, as I discuss in chapters 2 and 6, is influenced by many varying factors: continuing tradition, passing on a certain brand of cultural capital to the next generation, establishing boundaries between "us" and "them," and subscribing to a membership in an "Indian community." However, what marks all these deliberations is an attempt to negotiate their status as members of a population that even after almost sixty years in Britain is referred to as "migrant"—as is captured in the absurdity of the term "third-generation migrant," an epithet solely preserved to refer to the so-called visible migrants. The identity negotiation of this status through arranged marriages, which mark them as different, is done by adapting arranged marriages to new settings in Britain. This has resulted in a varied spectrum of matchmaking practices (see chapter 2), which allows for enacting choice and agency as prized ingredients in their identification as British Indians. Consequently, any subversion, translation, or reworking of arranged marriage practices in Britain points to a discourse that is uniquely British Indian—an ethnicity that is of much emotional and political significance to its bearer. By acknowledging the importance of the fluid, hybrid, and dynamic nature of identities, postcolonial theory also provides me with the scope for the acknowledgment of a particular kind of subjectivity, one that functions in an "interstitial passage between fixed identifications [and which] opens up the possibility of a cultural hybridity that entertains difference without an assumed or imposed hierarchy" (Bhabha 1994, 4). This sentiment about the possibility of entertaining difference without an assumed or imposed hierarchy has been the mantra that has guided the analysis of the data collected for this book. My concern has been not with defending or valorizing the practice of arranged marriage but with highlighting its diversity and significance in the enactment of a particular form of British Indian citizenship.

More importantly, as Sidaway (2002, 27) comments, "the multiple paradoxes of geographical 'encounters' with and 'explorations' of the postcolonial (in all its guises) can help us . . . to become aware of what it means to confront difference, to look again at what we think we know." As such, postcolonial theory helps me to approach the study of arranged marriage from a new vantage point that allows for the recognition of the diversity and complexity of this cultural practice among a people whose identities have been mediated by the traces, memories, and histories of more than two hundred years of British imperialism and resistance to it.

The Research Site and Participants: The British Indian Diaspora

The book is based on ethnographic fieldwork conducted over a five-year period in the North East of England, which is one of nine official regions of England. It covers Northumberland, County Durham, Tyne and Wear, and the area of the former county of Cleveland in North Yorkshire. For the purposes of my research, the term "first-generation migrant" refers to those who as adults migrated to Britain. Second-generation migrants are those who were born in Britain or were very young at the time of migration. All the first-generation migrants I interviewed had an arranged marriage. They had also arranged their children's marriage or were intending to do so. The second-generation migrants whom I interviewed either were married (through an arranged marriage) or were looking to marry in the near future. The participants varied in their age, period of migration, and social class. They ranged in age from twenty-one to seventy years old, and most were part of the Commonwealth migration wave of the 1950s and 1960s and had lived elsewhere in Britain before moving to the North East. They traced their origin to the states of Punjab, Gujarat, and Bengal in India. In terms of class makeup, there was an even split between working-class people running small businesses such as convenience stores or small restaurants and lower- to upper-middle-class people engaged in professional jobs as doctors, engineers, or teachers. Another group of participants were young professionals (ages thirty to forty) who came to the United Kingdom in the

1990s as part of the IT skilled migration program or as students to the region's universities. The selection of respondents from this group was intentional so that I could compare the perceptions of arranged marriage across two very different cohorts of first-generation migrants. The majority (60 percent) of the respondents identified as Hindu, with regional qualifications highlighted as Hindu-Punjabi and Hindu-Bengali. Sikhs (30 percent) and Indian Muslims (10 percent) made up the rest of the sample. All interviews were tape-recorded, and permission to do so was sought at the beginning of each exchange through informed consent. To ensure anonymity and confidentiality, all personal names have been changed to pseudonyms and any personal or identifying information provided by participants has been removed from the data. Where professional affiliation has been discussed, I have modified job titles and descriptions to nearest alternatives to avoid any loss of confidentiality. The resultant mix of participants can be illustrated as falling into the groups depicted in Table 1.

In this book I use the term "diaspora" to refer to Indian migrants resident in Britain. The term comes from the Greek word *diaspeirein*, meaning a scattering of seeds. Although the term has usually been restricted to refer to migrant populations who have suffered forceful expulsion from their homeland (classically used to refer to the Jewish diaspora), it has also found currency in describing the migrant condition in a postmodern world. It has been used to denote transnational movement in the age of globalization and the growth of non-nation-based solidarities in the contemporary period (Robertson 1992; Appadurai 1996). New notions of diasporic identities (in, for example, Hall 1990; Gilroy 1997; Cohen 1997; Brah 1996) and experiences have also emerged. The popularity of the term and its usage follows "a wider tendency to insert and promote a less essentialised and a more historically and analytically informed vocabulary into the traditional concerns of 'race and ethnic relations'" (Anthias 1998, 557). As a result, while for Gilroy (1997, 328) "diaspora is a valuable idea because [it is] . . . an alternative to the metaphysics of 'race,' nation and bonded culture coded into the body," for Said (1984) it is linked to the condition of exile. Hall (1990) has discussed the concept in relation to hybridity: "The diaspora experience as I intend here, is defined, not to be an essence or purity, but by the recognition of a necessary heterogeneity and diversity; by a conception of 'identity' which lives with and through, not despite, difference; by hybridity" (Hall 1990, 235).

TABLE 1

Profiles of the "Three Groups" of Participants Involved in the Research

Group 1	Group 2	Group 3
First-generation migrants (migrated in the 1960s) who had transnational arranged marriages with one spouse (usually wife) following the husband from India to Britain. The main professions included in this group were corner-shop owners (mom-pop stores in the US context), property developers, small enterprise owners, lawyers, medical professionals (doctors and nurses), academics, homemakers, tailors, and restaurateurs.	First-generation migrants (migrated in the 1990s) who also primarily had transnational arranged marriages (went back to India to find a wife or husband) with a small group of people who had married British-born Indians. This group included people with jobs as IT professionals, engineers, and academics.	Second-generation migrants (born and brought up in the UK or born in the subcontinent but grew up in the UK) who were married (to British-born individuals) because of an arranged match or were looking to get married. The professions represented in this group included corner-shop owners, property developers, small enterprise owners, students, shop assistants, housewives, restaurateurs, waiters, doctors, engineers, and teachers.

One of the most important distinctions of such a concept as diaspora is that it refocuses attention on transnational and dynamic processes of the construction and reproduction of identities in contrast to the fixed, determined notion of self-identity predetermined by place of origin and belonging. Consequently, it provides a useful analytic tool to understand identity formations in a globalizing world. Floya Anthias (1998, 559) provides an insightful analysis into the conceptual purchase of "diaspora" when used to refer to migrant communities. According to her, there are two main approaches to the way the concept has been used. She identifies the first approach with the work of Robin Cohen. In *Global Diasporas*, Cohen (1997) argued that there are six criteria for allowing the term "diaspora" to be used by and for a group of migrants: dispersal and scattering, collective trauma, cultural flowering, a troubled relationship with the majority, a sense of community transcending national frontiers, and promoting a return movement. Following from these criteria he constructs five different types of diasporic communities: victim, labor, trade, imperial, and cultural. He classified Indians under the "labor diasporic community" to acknowledge the legacy of the migration patterns of the Indian diaspora originating under British colonialism.

However, this schema is not very exhaustive, and if one were to use it simply as a typology to ascertain whether, for example, British Indians can constitute a diaspora, its gaps become apparent. All the criteria can at one time be a part of a diasporic experience for a person or a group and may not be so for some other members of the same group. So where collective trauma may be a part of the diasporic experience of Ugandan Asians who were exiled to Britain from East Africa, that is not the case for all British Indians. Furthermore, the Indian diaspora—which, as Amitav Gosh (cited in Clifford 1994, 285) has argued, "is not so much oriented to its roots in a specific place and a desire for return as around an ability to re-create a culture in diverse locations"—does not fit this typology, which is based on the cause of migration rather than its effect on both the migrants and their adopted country's society. The issue here is that using diaspora as a typology restricts its conceptual value by signifying a group as a "unitary sociological phenomenon" (Anthias 1998, 563). It leads to an assumption of a transnational community bonded by ethnic solidarity. Where this may be true in some cases, increasingly, as successive generations of migrants reach maturity in their parents' adoptive country, mere similarity and commonality of traditions are not what constitute their diasporic identity; more vital are their everyday negotiations living with difference. Thus, the very strength of the concept lies in its appreciation of the experience of difference and diversity among groups of people who have for varied reasons left their country of birth, and it is in this sense—*diaspora as a social condition and as a societal process*—that I use it in this book. To quote Anthias again (1998, 565),

> The diasporic condition is put into play through the experience
> of being from one place and of another, and it is identified with the
> idea of a particular sentiments towards the homeland, whilst being

formed by those of the place of settlement. This place is one where one is constructed in and through difference, and yet is one that produces differential forms of cultural accommodation or syncretism: in some versions hybridity. . . . Here issues around the destabilising effect of transition and movement of the individuals' cultural certainties may be explored and the ontological and epistemological effects researched.

Consequently, in the context of Indians in Britain it is their "cultural certainties" pertaining to the practice of arranged marriage that is explored in this book; I seek to understand how their "diasporic condition" aids or hinders their membership of postcolonial Britain. It is important to note here that for Anthias (1998) ethnicity and commonality of origin are the two major factors that underlie any discussion of diaspora. A preoccupation with these has led academics to not attend fully to "intersectionality," that is, to issues of class, gender, and transethnic alliances. She calls for overcoming this "ethnicity" problematic in order to better appreciate this concept and its resultant societal processes. To some extent, this book is an attempt to steer a more intersectional focus on arranged marriages, which is signaled by the usage of the term "British Indian diaspora" instead of, for example, "Indian ethnic community" and through an exploration of the intergenerational and gendered notions driving arranged marriage practices. My focus is on the practice of arranged marriages and how its practitioners encourage and at times discourage the flow of their cultures. In their most fluid form cultural practices encourage diasporic and transnational forms of belonging, while in others they might encourage a sentiment of preserving and fixing identity narratives, both of which are discussed in this book. Finally, Avtar Brah (1996, 183) made a case for understanding the diasporic identity of Indians in Britain as a "confluence of narratives." She contends that "the identity of the diasporic imagined community is far from fixed or pregiven. It is constituted within the crucible of the materiality of everyday life; in the everyday stories we tell ourselves individually and collectively." Thus, in this book the term "diaspora" is also used in its meaning as a *narrative in the making* of the journeys of migration that are told, lived, and retold in the promotion of a collective as well as an individual British Indian subjectivity.

Researching and Translating Your "Own Culture"

In analyzing the data and writing this book, I have translated responses from the participants' native Hindi and Punjabi (for first-generation and some second-generation migrants) into English—a language that is not my mother tongue. And if the quality of the research enterprise depends, as Silverman (2000, 19) has observed, on "the power of language to display a picture of the world," then a discussion on my use of English translations is warranted here. Temple and Young (2004, 164) have pointed out that "researchers have accepted to varying degrees the view that meaning is constructed in rather than expressed by language." Thus, by employing a discursive approach to arranged marriage, I have tried to capture the meaning-making exercise that is involved in creating particular kinds of interpretations of the practice. Since I translated interviews from Hindi, Urdu, and Punjabi to English, language became ever more significant as "there is no single correct translation of a text" because "almost any utterance in any language carries with it a set of assumptions, feelings and values that the speaker may or may not be aware of but the field worker, as an outsider, usually is not" (Temple and Young 2004, 164). All the first-generation respondents chose to talk in Hindi, Urdu, and/or Punjabi, while the second-generation respondents spoke in English. The colloquial expressions of the language of their region in India also frequently occurred in their speech. The more practical dilemma for me as a researcher was not only to ensure the credibility of the translation but also to preserve the essence and feel of the dialogue. I have tried to do this by providing idiomatic rather than literal translations. Doing so involved translating following the structure and grammar of English to preserve the meaning of the dialogue. Only when I could not find an equivalent in English was the Hindi or Urdu expression included in the text with a literal English translation in brackets. While this strategy helped me to provide the reader with a flavor of the dialogue exchange, it did not address the more profound questions of representation and the ethical and epistemological implications of translating from one language to another. Across disciplines, writers and researchers have been concerned with how language is used to construct representations of people in oral and written accounts. Here, however, I concentrate on the use of

English and the implications that it has for the way I chose to represent the stories of the participants.

Spivak (1992, 2003) demonstrates that language is not neutral, and translation is a subjective and political process. She sets up a politics of translation by arguing that current translation practice within academia is biased toward English language structures, which silence alternative ways of constructing the social world through language. As a way of countering this bias, Spivak (1992, 184) proposes that "the history of the language, the history of the author's moment, the history of the language-in-and-as-translation, must figure in the weaving [of the translation] as well." While a history of the language and translation is beyond the scope of this book, what is warranted here is "the history of the author's moment"—so what follows is an examination of my relationship with the English language. It is aimed at providing insight into the sensibilities that have guided the translation of the participants' speech and my interpretations of it.

I speak English with a good degree of competence. I can also speak Hindi, Urdu, and Punjabi. I would go as far as saying that sometimes I can write and express myself better in English than in Hindi. But English is not my mother tongue; it was not the language that my mother spoke to me when I was a baby. It is difficult to pin down what my mother tongue is because my mother did not speak to me only in Hindi but in a mixture of English, Hindi, and Kumaoni, her native dialect from the foothills of the Himalayas. She also insisted that no matter how well I learned to speak English or any other language it would never be *my language*; I would always speak Hindi in many languages. What I am trying to highlight here, at least on my behalf, is a lack of proprietary identity or oneness with the English language, which is a privilege perhaps exclusive to native users. Derrida (1996, 2) expressed the sentiment much more eloquently when he offered this lyrical refrain while discussing his relationship with the French language: "I only have one language; it is not mine . . . but it is not foreign to me." English is my chosen language of expression, but it is not mine; it is not regarded by many as such. I had to write tests to prove my competence in this foreign language when enrolling at the university where I study and work, but at the same time it is not foreign to me. I can say with as much certainty as is possible in such matters that I think, dream, speak, and write in a particular brand of English. Some, like my mother, may say it is an Indian brand, but I think it is not just Indian but a hybrid of particular sensibilities that arise because of my identifications, voluntary and involuntary, with the legacy and histories of British colonialism. Moreover, the relationship that I (and I suppose my respondents) have with English also carries the yolk of (post)colonial legacies.

English was the language of the Raj, and many Indians were taught the language to service the empire. Following independence, English, like many other remnants of colonialism, has stayed with us, although it has been Indianized. I have included this observation here to highlight my linguistic hybridity that is a result of my postcolonial condition, and consequently the translations, representations, and interpretations on which this book is based are a reflection of my respondents' and my personal relationship with the English language and its attendant colonial legacies. In keeping with this sentiment, I have highlighted Indian English neologisms such as "homely girl," "traditional-minded modern girl," "lookwise," Aunty Jis (see chapters 3 and 4), and "love-cum-arranged marriages" (see chapter 2) that were used by my respondents to describe the practice of arranged marriage. Moreover, I have approached the institution of arranged marriage from the perspective of my respondents who referred to a possible match as a *rishta*, a relationship (Shaw and Charsley 2006), to bring out the personal and intimate deliberations that are involved in the choice of partner. The Hindi/ Urdu word *rishta* literally means relation or relationships, but it more effectively captures the emotional and interpersonal register of arranged marriage practices in contrast to the mechanical sounding "arranged marriages." This approach allows me to appreciate the significance of the relationship (*rishta*) and identity making attributes of arranged marriages in contrast to the longstanding understanding of arranged marriages as a cold practice in need of change to a warm love marriage ideal. In the next chapter I turn to these *rishtas* by presenting the diversity of marriage practices that fall under the remit of the umbrella term "arranged marriages."

2

Becoming Modern and British

Enacting Citizenship through Arranged Marriages

This chapter presents a spectrum of arranged marriage practices that I found were prevalent among my respondents. It begins by discussing the problem of defining arranged marriages and shows that several matchmaking practices fall under its remit. I argue against a singular definition of this varied and complex practice and highlight the diversity of routes that can lead to an arranged marriage. Moreover, I make a case for understanding arranged marriages as a discursive practice—one that presents the British Indian discourse of marriage and family. I also argue that this discourse offers its practitioners opportunities to tailor this practice to position them with respect to a certain degree of modernity that they have chosen to embrace as British Indians. I also highlight how the various modifications that are made with respect to individual choice and romantic love are rationalized by my participants as signs of their commitment to enacting their own version of British Indian citizenship. Finally, I show how a paradoxical version of British Indian citizenship underlines the practice of arranged marriages whereby my participants formulate their sense of belonging and unbelonging to postcolonial Britain.

Arranged Marriages: Existing
Frames of Understanding

The notion of marriage occupies a paradigmatic status as the object of anthropological research, where marriage has been understood as "the definitive ritual and universally translatable regulative ideal of human societies" (Borneman 1996, 215). Definitions of marriage have variously focused on "sentiment and subjectivity, social or mental structures, or transactions and strategic choice" (Levine 2014). Marriage has been theorized as a structural institution (Radcliffe-Brown 1940; Leach 1961), as a postmodern relationship (Giddens 1992; Beck and Beck-Gernsheim 1995), and as a system aimed at preserving patriarchy and heterosexuality (Riviere 1971; Rubin 2009). Tovar (2001, 1301), writing in the *Routledge International Encyclopedia of Women*, defines marriage as "a culturally approved relationship that legitimizes a sexual and economic union, usually between a man and a woman." All states have definitions of what constitutes a legal marriage and under what circumstances it can be lawfully dissolved; indeed, there may be as many definitions of marriage as there are cultures and legislatures.

Therefore, the emphasis in current studies on marriage is not so much on defining marriage but on highlighting how marital institutions take various forms and analyzing them in relation to their social, economic, and cultural contexts (Gardner and Osella 2003; Constable 2005; Palriwala and Uberoi 2005; Gabb 2008; Morrison 2010; Fink and Holden 2010; Patico 2010; Yeoh 2013). Within this research, there exists a division between marriage forms that are a result of romantic love and marriage forms where romantic love is a result of the marital union. Moreover, as Khandelwal (2009, 584) has argued, "arranged marriage exemplifies the problem of exaggerated cultural difference"; consequently, scholars studying family and marriage among advanced economies privilege the notion of romantic love in heterosexual marriage with no reference to arrangement or strategic choice, while those who study marriage in the Global South or among minority populations in the West focus on arrangement and strategic choice with little emphasis on the affective register of such practices. As I have argued elsewhere (Pande 2014), this divide in marriage scholarship not only assumes the complete hold over the migrant of traditional gender and family norms by underscoring the foreignness of their cultural practices such as arranged marriages but more problematically contributes to the discursive portrayal of arranged marriages as certainly less than and other to mainstream marriage practices. As this chapter shows, instead of being guided by a rigid prescriptive definition of a universal arranged marriage, British Indians are increasingly flexible in their terms and references to this practice.

The *Oxford English Dictionary* defines arranged marriage as "a marriage the partners to which are chosen by others, usually their parents." This a good generalized characterization because it covers the essential ingredient that makes a marriage an arranged one: that is, the choice of a spouse is not an individual affair but is undertaken in consultation with parents, family members, and/or relatives. I have used this definition as a starting point for understanding this practice because unlike other definitions it leaves scope for examining it without any preconceived notions of the presence or absence of coercion. My research was conducted among people who had chosen to have an arranged marriage. Arranged marriages in this context can be best understood as a matchmaking practice where the prospective husband and wife are introduced to each other through family or friends. The decision to marry or to decline the match always rests with the two individuals involved.

In the extant literature, arranged marriages have been predominantly analyzed using the lens of transnationalism because traditionally arranged marriages, especially among first-generation migrants, involved a union between a British resident and a bride or groom from the Indian subcontinent. This has led to some scholars referring to arranged marriages as transnational marriages (Kibria 2012; Shaw and Charsley 2006; Shaw 2006; Charsley and Shaw 2006; Palriwala and Uberoi 2005). The field of transnational studies has provided us with a rich set of literature on the mechanics and motivations of arranged marriage practices. It has focused on consanguineous or cousin marriages (Charsley 2007; Kuper 2008), the politics of migrant rights and multiculturalism (Bonjour and de Hart 2013; Myrdahl 2010; Schmidt 2010; Gedalof 2007; Phillips 2007), and kinship relations (Ballard 1990, 2001). Closely related to this is the literature on the status and role of women in arranged marriage practices. The gender relations within arranged marriages have been critically examined by feminist scholars. This literature can be divided into two strands—the first strand has been instrumental in exposing the lack of agency available to women in transnationally arranged marriages (see, for example, Menski 1999, Abraham 2005, and Hall 2002 on immigration regimes and women's rights; Constable 2005, Lu 2005, and Blanchet 2005 on mail-order brides; Jeffery 1976,

Werbner 1986, and Shaw 1988 on Pakistani women and patriarchal marriage norms; Palriwala and Uberoi 2005, Sheel 2005, and Kibria 2012 on dowries and arranged marriages). The second strand has examined closely the complex gender dynamics within arranged marriages to show that women are not passive actors in the arrangement and matchmaking exercise (Donner 2002; Raj 2003; Sen, Biswas, and Dhawan 2011; Pichler 2011; Mukhopadhyaya 2012; Mohammad 2015; Pande 2015). This literature has illuminated the diversity of women's experiences of arranged marriages and the role they are able to play in them and has highlighted how women are actively involved in negotiations of arranged marriages and are able to exhibit choice and agency within what is still a largely patriarchal cultural setting. Noteworthy here is work by Ester Gallo (2005, 2006), who through her research with Malayali (from Kerala) women migrants in Italy has shown that far from always being a site of lack of agency, arranged marriages can also offer opportunities for the redefinition of gender relations as a result of women's pioneering status as migrants in Italy. Research by education scholars such as Bhopal (2009, 2011) has shown that although arranged marriages may bring with them an expectation of suppressing women's choices, increasing access to higher education for British Indian women has also meant that women can exercise more freedom and use their newly acquired social capital to facilitate a better match for themselves (Ahmad 2012). More recently, Robina Mohammad's (2015, 610) research with British Pakistani women raised in Birmingham also provides evidence of the ways in which transnational arranged marriage practices offer the potential to navigate and rework patriarchal gendered norms of marriage conventions. She argues that her informants' narratives "illuminate the intricate gendered geographies of intimacy [and] reveal the processes by which informants gain a sharper awareness of their own expectations for companionate marriage and intimacy. They read these expectations as underlining their difference from their spouses and as part of the assertion of modern, Muslim womanhood, cosmopolitan identities belonging firmly within the host nation."

The last point is particularly relevant to my research. It highlights the fact that even though marriage (of all kinds) is a "a bundle of rights" (Leach 1961) and a border-making union, it also involves opportunities for adapting the institution to personal goals and aspirations, and as Mohammad's research (2015) and this book show, among British Asians arranged marriages are being increasingly reconfigured to define their "modern" British identities.

In addition to this qualitative research on arranged marriages, there are also statistical studies discussing its varying rates and patterns as a measure of the assimilation of migrant groups to host societies; here marriage is referred to as "mate selection" and its cultural and social dimensions are not appreciated (see Korson 1969; Fox 1975; Gurak 1987; Xiaohe and Whyte 1990). For instance, Batabyal (2001; Batabyal and Beladi 2002, 2011) proposed econometric formulas to predict the likelihood and/or success rate of an arranged marriage. In his research, social factors were reduced to externalities and the people involved in an arranged marriage to variables or economic agents, which contributed to the portrayal of arranged marriage as a cold, rational strategy rather than also being the starting point of a companionate relationship between two people.

This is evident from a growing body of literature that focuses on the affective register of arranged marriage practices in India and among the Indian diaspora (Puri 1999; Parry 2001; Donner 2002; Fuller and Narasimhan 2008; Twamley 2014), in Pakistan (Donnan 1998), and in Sri Lanka (De Munk 1998). This literature has shown how there are various interpersonal factors involved in the practices associated with arranging a marriage and that there are several different routes into an arranged marriage. Some routes have been discussed by researchers examining arranged marriage practices among British Indians (Jhutti 1998; Raj 2003; Pichler 2011). They detail cases of arranged marriages where the prospective couple can "arrange to fall in love" while giving due consideration to their parents and their wider family's input in the choice of their spouse. My research builds on this literature to highlight the diversity of practices that fall under the term "arranged marriage."

While this literature has contributed significantly to our understanding of arranged marriages, there persists a surprising lack of clarity and coherence in the usage and interpretations of the term itself. Most often arranged marriages are not clearly defined, so forced, consanguineous, and transnational marriages are all clubbed under that term. There are considerable differences among all three: Forced marriages involve coercion and offer no opportunity to the prospective spouses in negotiating an arrangement of their choice. Consanguineous marriages primarily take place between South Asian Muslims (Shaw 2006). And not all arranged marriages are transnational, as many are arranged among partners resident in Britain (Shaw and Charsley 2006). This is increasingly the case among young British Indians whose ties to the country of origin are not as strong as they were for first-generation migrants. Therefore, while some arranged marriages may be transnational, not all are. Even though there is an acceptance of the dynamic and flexible nature of arranged marriage practices (Stopes-Roe and Cochrane 1990; Shaw 2006; Bhopal 2011; Ahmad 2006), the practice is often defined by implication or tacitly assumed to have an accepted definition. Although I am wary of crafting definitions when it comes to sociocultural practices, I believe that this lack of clarity in the understanding of the different forms of arranged marriages has foreclosed a more nuanced understating of the practices, leaving them exposed to pejorative stereotyping in the popular media and misinterpretations in immigration policy. In view of the negative connotations that the term "arranged" entails, some scholars have made calls to rebrand arranged marriages as "facilitated or assisted" marriages (Mukhopadhyaya 2012; Ahmad 2006). In my own research I have found at least four different types of matchmaking practices that compose what can be termed as "the spectrum of arranged marriage practices"; and as I argue later in the chapter, instead of defining arranged marriages it is more fruitful to understand them as a discursive practice.

The Spectrum of Arranged Marriages

In order to discuss the different forms of arranged marriage practices, it is first important to highlight the predominant understanding of arranged marriages that was prevalent among the British Indians involved in this research. This was presented to me as responses to the question "How would you describe the practice of arranged marriage to someone who had no idea of what it is?" The most common way arranged marriage was described was as a mode of matchmaking. This description was given by members of both the first and second generations. They described an arranged marriage as one where the prospective bride and groom are introduced to each other, usually by their parents or in some cases by members of the extended family.

After this it was up to the potential bride and groom to decide whether they wanted to go ahead with the match or not. Words like "facilitation" and "liaison" were used to describe the role of the parents, as is evident from the following quote: "Arranged marriage is when instead of people meeting themselves with a potential partner or taking the initiative to find someone . . . the family facilitates it. So they find potential partners for them and usually the parents look out for the best interest of their children. The marriage only takes place . . . when everyone is happy with a mutual agreement" (Gaurav). For Gaurav, parents, relatives, and friends are all involved in attempts to match a couple. The participants did not see a significant difference between arranged marriages and love marriages as they are practiced in the West, apart from the mechanism in which one meets one's future partner. So where Western couples may hope to meet their spouse in a pub or club, for British Indians this is done by their family members or friends in a formalized way. All the participants were unanimous in their understanding of arranged marriage as a mode of matchmaking in which "a cultural logic of desire" (Del Rosario 2005, 253) is administered and mediated by the self and the family. The cultural logic of desire or the idea of romantic love was regarded not as a foundation for marriage but as an ingredient in the making of a happy marriage. During my research I was able to identify at least four different ways in which the management of desire through arranged marriage was achieved. However, it is important to acknowledge here that arranged marriages incorporate a complex set of practices and discourses such that no two British Indian families can be said to do arranged marriages in exactly the same way, even though they all share certain common ideas about the practice. This will become evident in the following discussion of the spectrum of arranged marriage:

- Traditional arranged marriages
- Semi-arranged marriages
- Love-cum-arranged marriages
- Arranged weddings

At one end of the spectrum are traditional arranged marriages. All the first-generation British Indians admitted to having this kind of marriage, which involved their parents along with close relatives taking the lead in matchmaking. Both the men and women said that they had "chosen" each other by looking at photographs exchanged as part of the matchmaking practice. They were then encouraged to meet as part of a family lunch or afternoon tea in the full presence of family members from both sides. As Ramesh, a fifty-five-year-old corner shop owner, describes, "They say it is a meeting but in name only, we barely exchanged a word. . . . Priya [now his wife] was sat between my sister and mother and I was on the opposite end of the table, I just liked the look of her and when my mother asked me if she should confirm the match I said yes. . . . Actually she said in code if she should serve the sweets, you know *muh meetha karna* [literally sweeten the mouth, meaning do the honors] and I nodded!" Ramesh describes a typical matchmaking meeting, a well-orchestrated social event that also serves as the arena for the delicate negotiations that are involved in arranging a match, which I will discuss in detail in the next chapter. The would-be couple are not allowed to meet on their own because courting is frowned upon by the older members of the family. So a meeting is arranged where the social performance of seeing each other is conducted. The confirmation of the match is done with a degree of delicacy to ensure that the meeting does not come across as a business deal, hence Ramesh's mother speaking in code. Not all those who had a traditional arranged marriage had actually met each other; some had agreed to the match solely on the basis of photographs. The hallmark of this type of traditional arranged marriage was that the couple getting married had had no real contact with each other until the wedding was solemnized. The reason this was referred to as "traditional" was because such marriages are not practiced anymore. The first-generation migrants who had had this type of traditional arranged marriage were very clear in their insistence that their children were not expected to have this sort of traditional marriage. Their children's marriages were semi-arranged.

Semi- or partly arranged marriages come next in the spectrum and include those where a suitable match was decided upon in due consultation with the couple looking to get married; they met each other in the presence of family, and the wedding date was decided upon. After this the potential bride and groom were allowed to fall in love in the run-up to the wedding. My participants fondly remembered how they would go to the cinema or to restaurants, sometimes chaperoned by a sibling or friend. Some exchanged love letters or emails and celebrated weekly and monthly anniversaries of their "first meeting." In short, all the rituals of courtship were observed until the wedding date, which was seen as the climax of this exercise. Here love is gently encouraged. This courtship is not frowned upon by the family because the match has been approved by the parents. As Sraboni described, "You know after our parents had met and the marriage had been agreed upon, we did do our share of dating, Ajit [her husband] took me on many romantic dinners, where he would unsuccessfully try to play footsie with me under the table [blushes and laughs]!" All those who claimed to have gone through this version of arranged marriage confessed to being in love with their chosen partner by the wedding. Since they were functioning within the boundaries of caste, class, and religion in looking for a spouse, the marriage was deemed to be arranged. The potential spouses were matched and courtship was encouraged. The period between the engagement and the wedding was short, usually not more than three to six months.

However, traditional and semi-arranged marriages appear to be going out of fashion as more and more young British Indians choose to have what they called a love-cum-arranged marriage. This was how the majority of second-generation British Indians described marriage. They made a clear distinction between love and arranged marriage and professed to bring both together in this new form. They were free to choose whom they wanted to marry. The process of finding a spouse was described as meeting someone usually by chance (or through a setup via friends, which I detail in the next chapter) and then going through the courtship. This scenario was described as the process of being in love. Once they decided themselves that they were ready to get married, they went to their parents and asked them to take over the arrangement of the marriage. This involved the parents approaching their counterparts from the other side and finalizing the match. The chosen object of affection would have to be approved by parents or close relatives from both sides; parental consent was of paramount significance to both parties. My respondents agreed that while falling in love they had kept their parents' priorities of similarity in ethnicity, class, and religion in mind, as the following conversation with Alok and Kanta, two British Indians who said they had a love-cum-arranged marriage, highlights:

KANTA: Being honest here, the fact that he is Hindu Punjabi . . . and we have common family friends. These were definitely plus points. He is well educated as well as slightly older than me so he ticked all the boxes. Falling in love with him was not only natural but seemed the right thing to do. So yes when you look for a partner to marry you do look at the characteristics your parents would approve of.

ALOK: You have to look at everything as a whole. Is he good with my family, will they like him? Does he fit in and his views as well as the way he thinks about things . . . all matter.

They were very clear about the fact that they had fallen in love. They met at a friend's wedding and "went out" for a few months without the knowledge of their parents. This involved, as Kanta described, "normal love/dating," and then they decided to tell their parents and let them make further arrangements. However, while falling in love was important for the proponents of love-cum-arranged marriage, what was more important was falling in love with the right person. One could not just fall in love blindly but had to try to fall in love with somebody who would also be approved by their parents as a good match. So an element of self-censorship in the choice of a marriage partner was exercised. Thus, love-cum-arranged marriage was regarded not as a compromise but as the ideal to meet the desires of both the parents and the child. This was achieved by not only embracing the process of falling in love (Also see Fuller and Narasimhan 2008; Sen, Biswas, and Dhawan 2011; Raj 2003) but also actively socially engineering the process so that one fell in love with the right person—who would match the parents' criteria of a desirable partner, such as having a similar ethnic and religious background, among other requirements that I detail in chapter 4. The offspring's need to fall in love and to find their own spouse went hand in hand with the parents' desire to be part of this process. Both generations felt that their parents had an active role in their lives, and it was important to listen to the voice of experience in this very crucial decision of their adult lives. They also described this as the way in which tradition could live side by side with modernity, where the modern idea of love can be made to match with the tradition of arranged marriage. The majority of my participants also regarded this as the future of arranged marriage, the form in which it will survive among British Indians.

Finally, at the opposite end of the spectrum from traditional arranged marriages were arranged weddings. This was a term used to describe a marriage union where once one had fallen in love and decided to get married, instead of you making the arrangements with contributions from one's parents, the parents were in charge of all arrangements related to the ceremony. As Reshma described, "You see I let my parents especially my mum, dad, and my grandparents go to town with the wedding extravaganza. They threw me a lavish wedding and it was my way of letting them take part in the most important day of my life and their way of showing how much I meant to them. So they arranged it all and that is why my partner, who is Russian, says it was an arranged marriage as we did not do any of the arrangement."

The arranged wedding was described by its practitioners as a "thoroughly modern form of arranged marriages"—it could involve marrying someone from outside one's community but only with the approval of one's parents. In this way arranged weddings differed from Western forms of companionate marriage where parental approval is expected but not necessary. It was crucial that the parents approved of the choice of the spouse, as Rakhee, who was married to a white British man, said: "It was really important to me that my parents liked Dan [her husband], when I brought him to meet them for the first time—it was really hard—I was so nervous. It worked out in the end, my parents really liked him and could see us together as a couple, the fact that he is interested in Indian food and culture also helped." She had a lavish four-day Indian wedding in which her husband's family enthusiastically participated. Her husband's acceptance of Indian culture and the approval of her parents were crucial; Rakhee told me that she would have reconsidered her love for Dan if her parents had disapproved of her choice: "What does it say about the nature of my love, if I am willing to let go of the love of my parents of twenty-six years for the love of a man I have only known for just a year?"

For Rakhee, the arrangement in this type of marriage involved the approval of her parents, without which she would have not gone ahead with the marriage. Moreover, for the practitioners of arranged weddings, the rituals and festivities of an Indian wedding were very important because they symbolized to the wider Indian community the parents' support for

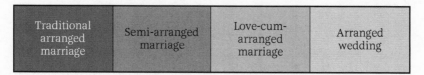

FIGURE 1. The spectrum of arranged marriage practices

marrying someone outside the community and also served as a way of welcoming the non-Indian family into the British Indian community.

WHAT IS CLEAR FROM THE ABOVE DISCUSSION is that within arranged marriages there exists a spectrum of practices: traditional arranged marriages, semi-arranged marriages, love-cum-arranged marriages, and arranged weddings (Figure 1).

In this spectrum, if traditional arranged marriage refers to a very prescriptive form of deciding on the match, arranged wedding represents the opposite end of the spectrum where the parents' role is restricted to providing their blessings to the couple along with their approval and financial support. The spectrum highlights the fact that these practices are not mutually exclusive or "types" in the strict sense of the word but rather exist on a continuum. Just like in an electromagnetic spectrum, all the different forms of marriage have their characteristic wavelength of "choice" and "arrangement," and depending on how these are valued in each family, arranged marriage can take any of these four shapes. When it comes to understanding choice, the fundamental choice was to have an arranged marriage or not. For some respondents whether they wanted to have an "arranged marriage" versus a "love marriage" was a significant choice allowed to them by their parents and family members. As Preeti explained, "I think the way I saw it was that either I would find somebody myself and have a love marriage and if I didn't, it would probably end up being an arranged marriage with the help of my parents." Following on from this, there is also the choice to say yes or no to the match proposed by one's parents or family. This is the crucial choice that all practitioners of an arranged marriage have to make. The two choices usually work in unison in the making of an arranged marriage. While the two descriptions of choice assume the person getting married is the main agent of making the choice, this was not always the case. Nearly all participants also talked about their "parents' choice," as is evident from the following quote by Gaurav: "Well I have to take into consideration my parents' choice as well. After all they are my parents, what about their wishes, their choice in who their daughter-in-law should be? My mum has always had a wish for a beautiful daughter-in-law whom she would treat as her own daughter; I don't have any female siblings you see." Thus, marriage is just not a matter of individual choice; one must also take into account the parents and their wishes. For Gaurav, his mother's desire for a daughter-in-law principally guided his decision to get married. Choice was not just personal judgment; instead, a decision was made in conjunction with the parents and immediate family. Hence, considerations of family approval, parental choice, and personal choice were all woven together in choosing a marriage partner via an arranged marriage. Indeed, this balancing act between individual and family choice is characterized by relations of power between the individuals getting married and the respective family members. So, for example, as I will discuss in chapters 4 and 5, the extent to which the marriage will be semi-arranged or involve consideration of romantic love is delicately negotiated by men and increasingly by women.

In addition to the question of choice, the degree and level of arrangement in an arranged marriage also vary depending on what sort of marriage practices a family favored. One of the distinguishing features of the way marriage is practiced in South Asian societies is the significance attributed to the arrangement. It is termed "arranged marriage" to signify perhaps the element of rational pragmatic arrangement that goes into its making. It is exemplified in the Indian argument that in a love marriage one falls in love and there is an element of spontaneity involved, while an arranged marriage is by design rather than by chance. Several of my participants pointed out how this understanding of arrangement as design, as planning one's choice of a life partner based on reason and pragmatism, was regarded as the main characteristic. Arranged marriages usually take place between members of similar social classes. Some emphasis on similarity of caste and common religion is regarded as the most important condition for the arrangement (Ballard 1990; Kalpagam 2005), as a key objective of arranged marriage is to decide on a match in a manner that does not disturb the structure of society where everyone knows their place in terms of religious affiliation and social class. Mixed marriages disturb this carefully ordered social milieu, which many thought was undesirable and made one "unsure of how to behave, as with one's own one knows what to do, what is the social code? But in mixed marriages it is all confusion too much mixing of culture, one doesn't know who one is anymore, all structure is gone" (Shanta). For those who choose to have a mixed marriage or an arranged wedding, arrangement principally referred to the coordination of the material aspects of the marital union, including the wedding and reception. Thus, depending on the various ways in which the two themes of choice and arrangement were understood, my participants tailored their arranged marriage in a way that best suited them and their family. The different meanings attached to "arrangement" and the value attributed to individual or collective choice vary between families and among members of the same family, resulting in personal ways of arranging marriages. This factor contributes to the making of a unique British Indian discourse of arranged marriages.

The Discourse of Arranged Marriages

In this section I delineate the view that arranged marriage is not a singular category but a discourse with varying definitions, values, and meanings attached to its practice. Most significantly, there are particular ways of talking about and describing the practice in relation to the various discursive domains that are associated with it. My examination of the different types of understandings (traditional arrangement, semi-arrangement, love-cum-arrangement, and arranged wedding) points to the existence of an array of views among British Indians. These span the spectrum of practices that are conflated under the term "arranged marriage." These forms exist as a discourse that reflects not only their views on arranged marriage but also the ways in which they have chosen to describe the process to me. I find a discursive approach to the practice of arranged marriage useful because it helps me to visualize this process of kinship "as identity work in action" (Lawler 2008, 32). It encourages me to appreciate the significance that is attributed to the practice by my participants in relation to their identities as British Indians. The focus on discourses of arranged marriage rather than on a definition of a "universal arranged marriage" (Puar 1995) makes it possible to acknowledge the various subjectivities, sensibilities, and personal attachments that are involved in the making of an arranged match. I borrow my understanding of discourse from Foucault (1972, 80), who discusses in *The Archaeology of Knowledge* that he uses "discourse" to refer to "the general domain of all statements, sometimes as an individualizable group of statements, and sometimes as regulated practice that accounts for a number of statements." By "the general domain of all statements" he refers to a group of statements that provide a language for talking about a phenomenon and a way of representing a particular kind of knowledge about a topic, such as a theological or colonial discourse. He also uses the term "discourse" to refer to "regulated practices that account for a number of statements," which refers to unwritten rules and structures in a society that allow the privileging of particular kinds of narratives over others. In the context of my argument, I use "discourse" to refer to both usages.

Arranged marriage has its underlying discourse in the way it is understood and talked about. There is the academic discourse that examines it, as I have discussed, from a transnational perspective; there is also a feminist stance on the patriarchal nature of the practice (Bhopal 2009; Mand 2005; Menski 1999; Abraham 2005). There is colonial imagery at play in the tabloid media that constructs people who have arranged marriages as parts of "traditional," "developing" societies in spite of the fact that some of them (such as my participants) might live and function in the "modern" and "developed" milieu of Britain. All these discourses fix the meaning of the practice as a singular phenomenon and by doing so also cement the identities of people who have arranged marriages. My findings about the spectrum of practices that fall under the rubric of arranged marriages deconstruct this idea by drawing out the heterogeneous nature of the practice.

In the context of the discourse of arranged marriage as "regulated practices that account for a number of statements" (Foucault 1972, 80), I refer to the various ways in which arranged marriages are practiced and the processes by which a match is decided upon. There is remarkable consistency in the way people choose to describe how marriages were arranged, as I will show in more detail in the next chapter. My participants highlighted a well-established routine of steps that was employed to look for a match. These involved, first, the parents approaching their son or daughter and asking them if they would like to have an arranged marriage or if they had somebody in mind already. After this, if the person agreed to their parent looking for a spouse, they "spread the word" (as one of the respondents put it) in the immediate social circle. This process might employ informal social networks of extended family and their contacts, more formal channels like a marriage bureau, an advertisement in the matrimonial section of the daily newspapers back in India, or a matrimonial website (Raj 2003; Mukhopadhyaya 2012; Titzmann 2013). Once some suitable matches were short-listed, a meeting was scheduled between the interested parties and the final choice was made.

However, the participants also admitted that in "real life" the elements of chance, destiny, and practicality played more significant roles than the "methods" that they had talked about in helping them to find a match. As such, I also interpreted the logistics of finding a match through an arranged marriage as a performative discourse that allows for the perpetuation of rituals and ceremonies surrounding the practice.

As Hall (1992, 291) discussed, "One important point about the notion of discourse is that it is not based on the conventional distinction between thought and action, language and practice. Discourse is about the production of knowledge through language. But it is itself produced by a practice: 'a discursive practice'—the practice of producing meaning. Since all social practices entail meaning, all practices have a discursive aspect. So discourse enters into and influences all social practices. Discourse is thus implicated in practice." It is also in this sense that I contend arranged marriage is a discursive phenomenon. It is formulated by its practitioners in terms of a group of statements about what the term "arranged marriage" means to them and their culture and identity. And as arranged marriage is indeed a practice (cultural, traditional, ethnic, whatever one may term it), central to its performance is a meaning-making exercise. There are two discursive domains under which this meaning-making exercise is performed: traditional and modern. The discourse of traditional arranged marriage serves two ends. First, it is used as a device to differentiate and set aside as "backward" the practice of forced marriage. Second, it is used to provide a referent to contrast with the ways in which modern arranged marriages (semi-arranged marriages, love-cum-arranged marriages, and arranged weddings) are practiced as in traditional versus modern arranged marriages. The discourses of traditional and modern arranged marriage were presented to me by the British Indians as their own way of understanding the practice, while the discourse of forced marriage was acknowledged to be how "others" see arranged marriage as a practice. The reason why this discourse was still prevalent even as most of my respondents claimed to have moved on to modern practices was blamed on certain "backward members of the Asian community who refused to change with the times" (Reema).

This particular way of visualizing arranged marriage helps British Indians first to construct an "other." In this case the other is defined as the media, the non-Asian majority in Britain, and also certain so-called backward members of Asian origin who insist on the practice of forced marriage. Second, it helps to define the boundaries between "us" and "them," *apana* and *paraya* in Hindi (ours/us—theirs/them). When a member of the "ours" (*apana*) talks about arranged marriage with little choice for the prospective bride and groom, they employ the term "traditional" as opposed to a foreign person's (*paraya*) view, which fixes arranged marriage as forced marriage. Last, the painstaking distinction between discourses of traditional and modern arranged marriages supports the construction of an identity as a people who have changed with time by embracing the modern ways of arranging marriages. The English words "traditional" and "modern" are employed to refer to how Asians resident in Britain have made the change from being of Asian origin to becoming British Indian.

The British Indian discourse of arranged marriage was marked by a conscious exercise of the characteristics of modernity. This is reflected in their conscious attempts to be seen as embracing and accommodating the needs of modernity in the exercise of arranged marriages in Britain. With respect to their parents' generation, the second generation portrayed themselves as more modern because they were not expected to have a traditional arranged marriage but could practice a more flexible semi-arranged marriage, love-cum-arranged marriage, or arranged wedding. They were keen to describe how they had chosen to exercise the very modern ideas of individual choice and agency to opt for what is seen as a traditional practice of arranged marriage. This was done by creatively interpreting the questions of choice and arrangement with reference to the individual as well as the collective self. The choice of a spouse was guided by individual choice and parental influence; a perfect match would accommodate both in a fine balance. They also chose to incorporate the demands of modernity such as the ideas of romantic love in their practice of arranged marriages. This tendency to reflect on one's biography in the context of becoming modern is the hallmark of what Eisenstadt (2005, 1) has referred to as "multiple modernities." He argues that although the West can be regarded as the origin of modernity, it is crucial to recognize that different cultures offer different pathways to modernity: "The idea of multiple modernities presumes that the best way to understand the contemporary world—indeed to explain the history of modernity—is to see it as the story of continual constitution and reconstitution of a multiplicity of cultural programs" (Eisenstadt 2005, 2). This view has an important implication for understanding modernity (Blunt and McEwan 2002; Kothari 2008; McFarlane 2011), namely that modernization and Westernization are not identical and that Western patterns of modernity are not the only authentic modernities.

What this points to is a way of embracing modernity where the traditions of the past are intermeshed with the demands of the present. In the case of British Indians, this is manifested in nostalgia for the past in terms of continuing the practice of arranged marriage but at the same time ensuring it suits the realities of their present as residents in a (post)modern society. This is apparent in the various adaptations made to traditional arranged marriage practices that were marked by aspirations for selective features of Western modernity such as romantic love and a certain degree of choice. In contrast to a secular and individualized Western sense of self, the British Indian approach to modernity was more in line with a desire for an identity that could be described as a progressive self but within the limits of religious and community boundaries. This self tries to shoulder the modern and the traditional simultaneously in a conscious attempt at integrating with British society and Western modernity at large.

In the South Asian context, Gerd Baumann (1996, 209–215) distinguishes between two forms of discursive practice—dominant and demotic. The dominant discourse reifies community and culture as essences by employing currently accepted divisions between South Asian and British settlers, based upon religious affiliation and nationality. The demotic discourse transgresses these divisions in everyday life. He argues that in particular young South Asians create a shared popular culture across these major divisions, fusing their identities as South Asian, through popular cultural aesthetic forms. They intentionally subvert the normative bound-aries of "community" set by parents. Nevertheless, the same people who use demotic discourses revert to the dominant discourse on public occasions (Baumann 1996). In the case of arranged marriages, it is not just a matter of practicing a demotic discourse in private and then reverting back to a dominant, more powerful discourse in the public arena. The transgression does take place as people acknowledge that they have an arranged marriage because it is part of their culture (a dominant discourse of South Asian culture), but they do it on their own terms as various interpretations of "choice" and "arrangement" come into play. The point is, as Madood, Werbner, and Werbner (1997, 18) argue, that this flux between the dominant and demotic discursive practices helps in "constituting a dual discursive competence that renders 'culture' and 'community' active terms of debate and negotiation in everyday life or vis-à-vis the local state. They draw on common sense ideas to objectify culture, community, and ethnos and even 'race' as self-evident homologues, while at the same time being aware of the remaking, reshaping and re-forming these very terms in other contexts."

Moreover, the insistence of British Indian second-generation migrants to enter into an arranged marriage, which puts them in contrast to main-stream British cultural practices, can be read as an example of what Stuart Hall (1996), while theorizing the evolution of black identities in Britain, termed "new ethnicities." He argues that they are emblematic of a new politics of representation—one that has arisen as a result of an awareness of the Asian experience (in this case) "as a diaspora experience, and the consequences which this carries for the process of unsettling, recombi-nation, hybridization and 'cut-and-mix'—in short the process of cultural diaspora-ization" (Hall 1996, 447). This new cultural politics of ethnicity is apparent in the "cut-and-mix" ways in which traditional arranged marriage practices have been refashioned as semi-arranged marriages, love-cum-arranged marriages, and arranged weddings to suit British Indian identi-ties. Furthermore, the repeated refrain of the respondents to differentiate "backward practices of forced and traditional arranged marriages" from their chosen forms of "modern" arranged marriages can be understood as enacting the British elements (associated with choice and romantic love) of their identity. The focus of my respondents on recoding arranged marriage as a practice marked by the conscious exercise of embracing a kind of modernity can be read as an affirmation of their desire to highlight the contestations over what it means to be British *and* Indian. Here the notion of enacting citizenship (Isin and Nielson 2013) is helpful in illuminating what could be termed the hybridization of arranged marriage discourses among British Indians. The concept of "enacting citizenship" understands citizenship not as something you have but as something you do. It extends the analytical purchase of the concept of citizenship beyond its study as a formal status to the realm of the informal (not recognized by the nation-state) acts of citizenship by migrant populations. This may include populations whose official document of citizenship may not always mirror the citizenship claim of its bearer, as was the case with my respondents who laid claim to citizenship as British Indian while holding a formal British passport, or it may also include performances of citizenship from people who have been denied a formal claim to citizenship (Tyler and Marciniak 2013). For British Indians, the different ways in which they claim to modify and modernize traditional arranged marriage practices were reflective of something more than the natural evolution of this cultural practice—it was a conscious act of laying claim to a British identity and performing British citizenship, as Prema argued: "We don't do arranged marriages like they do back home in India, we are also British, we have more choice and freedom." The spectrum of arranged marriage with the different degrees of choice and agency that it affords is seen as evidence of their commitment to the modern values of their country of residence. For their practitioners, arranged marriages are not regarded as antagonistic to the British way of life but are an essential component of a British Indian identity. However, this enactment of British Indian citizenship happens against the backdrop of a wider public and policy discourse that renders arranged marriage as an outdated practice and threat to liberal British values. This sets the practitioners of arranged marriage on a collision course with the majority culture, which my participants were keen to highlight: "We will never belong, you can never be English." Indeed, what emerged from their dogged insistence on enacting a modernized version of arranged marriages, to portray themselves as more British while also lamenting the fact they will never really belong to Britain, is a paradoxical sense of belonging to postcolonial Britain. Modifications to traditional arranged marriages create a temporary and fragile sense of doing *your duty* as a *British* Indian while also knowing that it may not be enough to allow you to fully belong, which in turn means that you don't let go of the Indian aspect of that identity. As I show later in this book (chapter 6), the pull of belonging to and preserving Indian culture is strong for British Indians and is partly the reason why arranged marriage has not given way to full Western-style love marriage. Having explored the different types of arranged marriages, in the next chapter I detail how marriages are arranged by highlighting the rituals and family traditions that constitute the matchmaking practices favored by British Indians.

3

Continuing Traditions as a Matter of Arrangement

> I think you should have a chapter in your book describing in detail how we arrange marriages and how intricate and wonderfully cultural a phenomenon it is. Not like the West where you just produce a person from somewhere and tell your parents that this is who you plan to marry.

The above excerpt is from an interview I conducted with Dr. Sraboni Das, a GP in the local medical practice. She had lived in Britain for thirty years, and both her sons partook in arranged marriages. She was regarded by many of my participants as a leading member of the local British Indian community—an independent woman with a career and family. Like her, nearly all the people I interviewed mentioned at least once during the interviews that they were frustrated with the lack of knowledge among non-Indians about what arranged marriages are, how they are arranged, and the continued confusion with forced marriages in Britain. It was Dr. Das who suggested that I devote a chapter to the "delicate process of arranging a marriage"—so in addition to analyzing how marriages are arranged among the British Indian diaspora, I fulfill her request in this chapter. I discuss the steps involved in arranging a match and highlight its key traditions. I argue that being seen to follow the different traditions and rituals associated with arranged marriage was central to my respondents' attempts at creating a home away from home in their adopted country. They did this by relying on their own memories of those traditions as they were practiced back home but also on the ritualistic script provided by the representations of those traditions in Bollywood films that help provide a reference point for ceremonies that were used in arranging a marriage.

As discussed in the previous chapter, people may have differing conceptions of what arranged marriage means to them, but they all share a common understanding of how the process of arranging a match takes place. They discussed with me in near formulaic sequence the well-established steps that needed to be followed. This process begins with the parents (or an aunt or uncle) checking if their son or daughter is ready to get married. In the past, arranged marriages were regarded as the default option, but this was no longer the case, and I was told that most parents checked first if their children were ready to get married and second if they wanted an arranged marriage. Readiness was rarely expressed directly by the person wanting to get married but was tested by the parents and confirmed at set milestones such as after college graduation, at the start of their first job, or after the wedding of an older sibling or friend. After confirming that their child wanted an arranged marriage, the parents "spread the word" in their social circle. This process ranged from employing informal social contacts to more formal channels like hiring a matchmaking agency, placing an advertisement in the nonresident Indian (NRI) matrimonial section of the daily newspapers back in India, or using a matrimonial website. This was all done with a set of criteria (agreed between the parents or family and the son or daughter getting married, which I discuss in detail in the next chapter) in mind about what would make a good match. Once some suitable matches were found, a meeting was scheduled between the interested parties and the final choice was made. This generalized process can be said to take place in two distinct phases, which I will discuss below:

In search of a partner: when the decision to have an arranged marriage is made and key informal and formal agents and channels are mobilized to find a good match based on mutually agreed criteria

Meeting the parents, the family, and the prospective spouse: when the first meeting between the prospective husband and wife and their families takes place and a final decision is made

It is important to note that the first phase applied only to those who decided to have a more traditional arranged marriage, where parents were entrusted to start the search. For respondents who reported having a more modern interpretation of arranged marriages, the first phase did not apply; however, they did observe the second phase, "meeting the parents." Indeed, taking part in this ritual was seen as the primary marker making their marriage arranged.

In Search of a Partner: "Spreading the Word"

The English expression "spreading the word" came up repeatedly as a key phrase encapsulating the early stages of the process of arranging a marriage. It involved first letting one's network of family and friends and the wider British Indian community know that the search had begun. Second, it involved mobilizing networks to find a suitable match. While increasingly more formalized networks are being employed, the start of the process was signaled through more coded expressions, as Ramesh, a fifty-eight-year-old semiretired teacher told me: "It is the word *chinta* [worry] that I started using a lot, so I would say to my friends, I have started to do *chinta* about Rahul's [his son] future, we need to find a wife for him. They would completely understand what I meant." Other expressions were also used, such as asking friends "to start thinking about my son or daughter" or to "keep in mind" the search. This notion that the search for a match needed to occupy the collective consciousness of the family and wider community, whether encapsulated in the sense of *chinta* (a feeling of care and worry) or in a request to "think about" a match, was regarded as a crucial step in the process of matchmaking. It helped in setting up arranged marriages as a shared community enterprise and reinforced a sense of belonging to the British Indian diaspora. In addition, other more discrete channels were also used; I have arranged them in increasing order of degree of formality:

- Aunty Jis networks
- Matchmaking friends
- Temple/gurudwara gatherings
- Matrimonial advertisements
- Matrimonial websites

Aunty Jis Networks

For people from the Indian subcontinent, any female relative or family friend other than those from one's immediate family is referred to as an aunty. The real aunty and uncle (one's parents' siblings) are referred to using the Hindi words *chacha/chachi* and *mama/mami*. All other male and female acquaintances of one's parents are referred to as aunty or uncle. The term *Ji* is a Hindi/Urdu honorific, like the English mister or miss, but it is a gender-neutral term. *Jis* is the plural form (Anglicized by adding *s*). As Reema, a twenty-seven-year-old schoolteacher undergoing an arranged marriage, explains, "The Aunty Jis network always works. They know my parents are looking for me so they will talk about this—such and such is looking for a bride or groom for their son or daughter—they will know who the other eligible people in the community are. They will come back to the family suggesting matches, may even work as a go-between between the two families if you decide to go ahead with their suggestion." Here Aunty Jis network is used to refer to female acquaintances but more specifically to those who are either housewives or retired from work. They are known to meet daily to chat and gossip about friends and family. They are the ones who know the comings and goings of households in the neighborhood and are sometimes caricatured as the local busybodies (Qamar 2017). Moreover, when my participants referred to their neighborhood, they meant not just the people living near their house or on their street. For most British Indians, anyone of Indian heritage living in the far corner of the town or city, maybe even a bus journey away, would count as a neighbor. It was not actual geographical proximity but shared cultural background that determined who a neighbor was. This is not to say that my respondents did not interact with their actual neighbors, but in the context of spreading the word for an arranged match, where considerations of commonality in terms of religion and ethnicity were paramount, the idea of neighbor was exclusive to Indian acquaintances and friends.

"Aunty Jis," who formed part of this imagined neighborhood, were seen as the ideal candidates for advertising the fact that one's daughter or son had agreed to get married and that "one was looking." Once these aunties are told to look for a match, they get to work, sharing the news with their network of friends and maybe even suggesting possible matches. This way of looking for a match thus relies on the assumption that there will always be in the immediate community one or two women, if not a large network of elderly aunties, who are the local gossips and may even practice matchmaking as a hobby. Contact with the Aunty Jis network is made rather informally—no one formally visits an aunty to outline the kind of a match one is looking for. It is taken for granted that once one starts dropping hints to friends and neighbors, the news will be transmitted by the Aunty Jis network. In fact, they might get in touch even before any such intentions are shared, much to the chagrin of a daughter or son who might not be ready to get married. It was also pointed out to me that while the parents or elders of the family valued the Aunty Jis for the social capital that they brought to matchmaking, they also practiced a degree of caution when taking suggestions for possible matches. As Mrs. Singhvi, an Indian lady whose son had been married as a result of a match made through the Aunty Jis network, said, "You see one has to know whose *rishta* [match] to take seriously. So, for example, I know that Kamala Aunty is a big gossip and is no judge of character, her own son has a failed marriage. I would never take her suggestion very seriously. . . . You know these things by experience." Here, the person who proposes the *rishta* must have a certain standing in the community. The fact that Kamala Aunty was seen as a poor matchmaker was partly because her son was divorced. The general attitude toward this kind of matchmaking and especially the use of the Aunty Jis network differs across the generations. The younger generation usually mocked them, and being called an Aunty Ji for one's dress sense or social skills was seen as an insult among the younger female British Indians. However, they did begrudgingly accept that these networks were the most efficient means of spreading important news among one's acquaintances, especially if one was looking for a match.

Matchmaking Friends

Matchmaking done by friends was the opposite of the Aunty Jis network. Where the latter were favored by the older generation and had a reputation of "the snooping neighbor," the former were preferred by the younger generation.

According to Munir, who self-styled himself as a matchmaking friend, "You see friends . . . like I am one. Doesn't it happen to you sometime that you meet somebody in a party and think this person will be perfect for my sister's friend or something like that? You know, not formal matchmakers but ones who keep their single friends in mind." Matchmaking friends would usually be people concerned with looking for a match for their single friends. What is interesting here is that while the Aunty Jis network was an entirely female bastion, the matchmaking friend could be a male or a female friend. More than once it came out in interviews that male colleagues or acquaintances would suggest prospective matches. They were also referred to as well-meaning friends when the matchmaking advice was unsolicited. Also, as Munir explained to me, "If one did not accept the match, one would usually say . . . they mean well but it is just not for us."

However, if the matchmaking was welcomed, the friends would go a step further to allow the possible match to meet. They might throw a party and invite the members of the prospective match and then contrive a meeting. Or they might be more forthright and suggest a match directly. Here again one's good intentions are valued. A person who is a good friend and "is looking out for you and your family" would be counted as a "well-meaning" friend, especially if the match does not materialize.

Temple/Gurudwara/Church Gatherings

These are informal meetings of families looking for a bride or a groom. They are sponsored by the Hindu or Sikh temple trusts and are the British Indian equivalent of a speed-dating event. Meetings are usually organized over a buffet lunch or afternoon tea. Nitin, a twenty-nine-year-old doctor who had met his wife at one such meeting, explains,

> It is this meeting that is usually organized by people at the temple where all Gujaratis will go and the motive is to get to know the people of your community and also to meet like-minded young people from your own community. I know it sounds really strange, I thought the same when my mother suggested going to something like this but believe me after a few awkward things like registering at the desk and wearing a name tag it was quite easy. I met Neela, my wife, over the water fountain where she was talking to her friend and was complaining how bizarre this whole charade was.

This kind of *shaadi mela*, which translates as "marriage fair," is like a conference of people looking to get married and their parents. They are usually community-based events, so Gujaratis have conferences for fellow Gujaratis, Punjabis for fellow Punjabis. I was told they were more common in cities like Leicester and Birmingham because of a larger number of Asians living there. This option was preferred by many second-generation respondents as it was seen as a relaxed way of finding out more about prospective matches away from the prying eyes of parents and family members.

Matrimonial Advertisements

Most newspapers in the subcontinent carry a supplement titled, for example, "Times Matrimony" or "HT Matrimony," named after two widely circulated dailies in India, the *Times of India* and *Hindustan Times* (*HT*). These have two sections: one for brides and the other for grooms. The layout is quite similar to the "lonely hearts" column of UK newspapers. The advert or "profile" as it is called is usually a twenty- to fifty-word description of the person who is looking for a match and some information about what kind of partner they are seeking. Here are three examples of matrimonial advertisements from the *Times of India*:

> Alliance invited for London based well settled Sikh, ramgariah boy, clean shaven, fair, smart, handsome, 29/61, MBA from IIM-C, working for leading management consultancy firm, looking for a smart beautiful, slim and educated girl. Reply with photo and bio-data.

> Alliance invited from handsome fair srivastava industrialist 25/5.10. Professionally qualified from top UK University belonging to reputed family running internationally famous business. From beautiful, well-educated girl of cultured family. Girl is only consideration. Sub caste no bar. Early marriage.

> UK based Dhiman Brahmin family match seeks suitable match for their daughter 26. 5.5, fair, slim, intelligent, B.tech, MS (USA) SW, working Microsoft UK on permanent visa. Boy should be suitably qualified, vegetarian, non-smoking from respectable north Indian family. Caste no bar, send BHP.

All these were placed under the "NRI matrimony" section of the paper, referring to nonresident Indian (NRI). The description involves the caste (Dhiman Brahmin) or the surname (Srivastava) and the age and height of the prospective groom or bride. BHP refers to biodata, horoscope, and photograph, which are usually requested by interested parties. The use of unconventional short forms such as BHP is a device to save money as the papers charge per word. There is a whole world of status and criteria condensed in these short adverts, and the research interest in this practice has been long-standing. There is a variety of literature (Upreti 1954; Chakrabarti 1974; Sharda 1990; Dugar et al. 2008) devoted to the analysis of matrimonial adverts, ranging from content analysis to the sociological consideration of caste and subcaste as criteria for a match and even the peculiar Indian English lexicon in which the advert is scripted (Kachru 1983). I found that the use of matrimonial advertisements was more common among young professionals who migrated to Britain in the 1990s usually on their own and had their immediate family still living in the subcontinent. The newspaper matrimonial was also popular among Indian Christians who do not have a large community base in Britain and as such cannot make use of a local network of family and friends.

Matrimonial Websites

The print-based matrimonial advert has given way to a more user-friendly internet-based version; these matrimonial websites are becoming increasingly common. Some popular websites are Bharatmatrimony.com and Shaadi .com. The major component of these websites is the profiles, and their services are similar to those offered by online dating websites. A typical profile comprises a photograph and some very specific information relating to caste, religion, ethnicity, education, employment, dietary preferences (vegetarian or nonvegetarian), and physical appearance. Nearly all websites present information such as primary details like name, age, height, and weight, even blood group, skin complexion, and mother tongue. This is followed by information about religion, caste, subcaste, horoscope, and eating and drinking habits. Education and professional qualifications follow next, where apart from the degree and current occupation, the monthly salary is also included. The websites also ask visitors to write a short personal note describing themselves and their expectations for a prospective partner. Visitors to these websites are provided with a choice of browsing through the existing profiles and looking for prospective spouses or making one's own profile as a potential bride or groom. Websites like Bharatmatrimony.com also offer filters that automatically restrict access to people with certain "types of profiles" from viewing your details. For instance, if one person had registered their profile with caste as no bar (meaning that caste is not an issue in their choice), they would be restricted from viewing profiles of those who have defined caste as one of their variables for choosing a spouse. This is optional but points to the degree of exclusivity these websites offer to their customers. The younger generation preferred to use matrimonial websites, although it was interesting to see that the actual website profile was nearly always set up by their parents; very rarely did the person getting married write their own profile. Moreover, the websites have a tab that allows users to see who uploaded the profile—the parents or the individual looking to get married. While it may seem inconsequential to an external observer, this information was seen as a useful filtering criterion; profiles created by parents were seen as more genuine and, as one of my respondents put it, "more respectable." Those set up by individuals were seen as being too similar to a dating website, as Reema said: "Well you know if they are seriously looking to get married only if the parents are involved, if not then they might just be the creeps that are on all dating websites."

Needless to say, what came across clearly in all the different channels used to find a prospective match was the close involvement of the parents or, in their absence, the other elders in the family. Even though the person getting married claimed to have the eventual choice in deciding whom they got married to, they deferred to their parents when starting the process. While some channels such as the Aunty Jis network and newspaper adverts (regarded as old-fashioned) were accepted by the younger generation to appease their parents, others such as matrimonial websites, recommendations from close friends, and temple/gurudwara gatherings were actively embraced by them as useful ways to begin the search for a partner. Once these channels had been utilized, most families reported drawing up a short list of suitable candidates who would be invited to meet the parents and the wider family.

Meeting the Parents, the Family, and the
Prospective Husband/Wife

One of the key rituals of the practice of arranging marriages is the first meeting between the prospective bride and groom and the members of the families. It is organized with such customary detail and ceremonial flare that it resembles the prescribed order of a religious ceremony. However, as will become clear in the following discussion, the prescriptive nature of this meeting is not always the result of an Indian religious and cultural code but is a direct import from meetings portrayed in Hindi cinema. Nearly all respondents grudgingly accepted that "this meeting" was more of "a modern tradition, as how they do it in the films" (Mr. Shukla). "The meeting," as most respondents referred to the occasion, took place after one had decided on a suitable boy or a good girl and was going to meet the family and the prospective match (see chapter 4 for details about how these are defined). The first meeting between the families has been immortalized by Hindi cinema, in which almost every romantic comedy features the meeting, which is now an institution among people from the Indian subcontinent. A typical meeting involves the families agreeing to get together usually at the woman's parents' house or in some cases in the home of a close relative or family friend. At times this meeting can also be held at the house of the person instrumental in the match, a friend who had set them up or an Aunty Ji who helped "spread the word." This is usually over afternoon tea in which the woman getting married is expected to showcase her culinary skills. The prospective groom's family that visits usually numbers around five or six people, depending on how many siblings the groom has. A grandparent or a family elder is nearly always included. A similar group can also be expected from the woman's side.

The meeting begins with the woman's parents welcoming the man's family in their house, then all sit down for tea. The woman is asked to stay in her room until called for. And it is after the formalities of introducing each other that the woman's father or mother calls for her. She typically arrives bearing tea, coffee, or other drinks. During this time the future mother-in-law may ask some direct questions of her or might indirectly try to gauge her personality. After this the potential bride and groom may be asked to go out to a different room or outside space for a chat. Sometimes they may also be encouraged to go for a drive or a walk, but always chaperoned by a cousin or friend. The meeting is organized "so that the girl and boy can meet each other and decide" and so the parents can also "check their house and standard of living." Every detail of the woman's household is scrutinized, from "the state of their curtains to the condition of their bathroom." As Mrs. Singhvi, who had been to many such meetings in the course of getting her four children married, explains,

> Well the meeting is your opportunity to find out whether the family you are marrying your daughter into or bringing a daughter-in-law from is compatible with yours. So there are certain things I always look for, the girls family should make an effort to impress us but not try too hard as well. . . . You know what I mean . . . like when we went to meet Sheela [her daughter-in-law] and were sat down over tea talking, the neighbor's little daughter came in and said standing at the door, "My mummy is asking when will you be finished with her Wedgewood china as we are expecting guests later" [laughs]. You should have seen the look on everybody's face. But you see I did not mind, I liked the fact that they had made an effort to impress us but had not gone beyond their means to buy a new tea set which would just have been too much [laughs].

Mrs. Singhvi's almost Jane Austenesque account of the meeting captures one of the more significant aspects of this ritual—that both the parties involved in arranging the marriage are aware of its performative nature. Nearly all my respondents agreed that it was rehearsed to the point that the meeting seemed like a well-orchestrated performance that, if you were able to pull off, could result in successful matchmaking with the two parties agreeing to the match. They know and, in some cases, expect the other party to put on a show that highlights the family and its status to a high standard in an effort to impress each other. With this knowledge in mind they then engage in a kind of game where both sides are waiting for minor slip-ups (such as in the account above) and other revelatory moments when the "real" nature of the family is revealed. All my respondents had stories of *meetings gone wrong* where they were able to see the more authentic face of the family, which would help them to decide if they wanted to go ahead with the marriage. These stories then became part of the "love story" of the couple concerned when they reminisced and reflected on their first meeting.

I spoke at length with my second-generation respondents about their experience of this meeting. While the men admitted to feeling nervous, they worried most about rejection rather than their performance at the meeting itself. Amol, who had gotten married two years ago after one such meeting, said, "I was nervous, yes I was, but I was also worried sick, what if the girl rejected me, that is not a nice feeling although I would say it is harder for the girls . . . all that filmi drama." Amol's sentiments here are representative of how the majority of my male respondents reported feeling about this meeting—a little nervous and worried about being rejected, but overall they also agreed that there was more pressure on the women to look and behave a certain way. As I have described above, the onus of performance of a dutiful daughter and prospective daughter-in-law was on the woman getting married. As Pratima, who had recently been through the experience, having been married some nine months previously, describes, "Oh it was just horrendous, the whole thing was so stressful. My mum must have made me try on ten saris, this regardless of the fact that I had never ever worn a sari before. They asked me to wear contact lenses. I can't cook, but they passed off samosas and pakodas bought from a restaurant as my creations [laughs]."

This expectation of presenting yourself as a prospective bride to portray traditional qualities of an ideal Indian woman (such as being a good cook, wearing traditional Indian clothing) was reported by all my female respondents. This presentation of the self as a "good girl" formed the central criterion through which British Indian womanhood was defined, and I devote the next chapter to examining it in more detail.

When I asked my female respondents how they felt about being scrutinized and judged on the basis of their appearance, many admitted to feeling awkward. As Pratima explains further, "I will say it is the most difficult exam I have ever taken, and I have studied medicine and even my fourth year viva wasn't as nerve-racking as this. It is something you can't prepare for, I was born a certain way and have grown up to be a certain type of person but for this one meeting you have to fit the mold." When I asked her if she had ever wanted to challenge these patriarchal expectations, she said that it was "part of our culture" and "so there was no point in kicking up a fuss about not doing this or that." Some other respondents equated the performance in the meeting to the Western practice of going on a blind date, when one dresses up to look one's best and performs to some extent to impress the other person. Most respondents justified the continuing popularity of this quaint practice in the name of preserving traditions. They also stressed the fact that their decision to agree to the match was not merely based on this meeting. There were different things that people said they liked or disliked on meeting the prospective match and that influenced them later to decide yes or no. In most cases they were not under pressure to make up their mind at the meeting. The decision of whether they felt that the match would be suitable was communicated after the meeting, usually within a week. Either party, the man or the woman, was allowed to accept or reject the match. Several such meetings would take place with different individuals until the desired match was found.

On being asked what made them decide to agree to the match, respondents evoked different reasons, ranging from as vague as "I had a good feeling about him" to quite definite ones like "she fit all our criteria of beauty and a good character." Many respondents also talked about how some of them had a list of questions to ask each other. Some of the standard questions were about the other person's hobbies and plans for their career. Noor, a twenty-three-year-old schoolteacher who had recently gotten engaged to a man she was introduced to by her mother and had been through the ritual of this meeting, explains,

NOOR: You see . . . I did not take this meeting as a burden, I knew I was expected to behave in a certain way but also knew that this was my chance to find out whether I wanted to marry this man or not. So when we were asked to go into the garden for a chat [laughs], just the two of us. I talked quite freely and candidly about who I was, both of us knew that in front of our parents we were behaving in a certain way, like I was being all demure and girly while in reality I am a right chatter box. I told him this and he seemed to like me.

RAKSHA: So what was it that made you decide that this would be the guy?

NOOR: To be honest, it was none of those things like what job he had or how he looked. He had a good job so it was a plus, but in reality he did remind me a lot of my dad who passed away when I was a sixteen.

I know it sound really pervy but you know what I mean, my dad was a good man, he kept us all so happy and so I have always wanted to marry a man like that and Aslam fit the bill. He still teases me for this but I know I made the right choice [laughs].

Noor points out that it was at the meeting that she decided to marry Aslam, and her decision was based on her personal emotions and the model of her father who had passed away. While for her it was the emotional dynamic between her and Aslam that convinced her to agree to an arranged marriage with him, for others the decision can involve more pragmatic concerns. For instance, Mrs. Singhvi pointed out how she did not mind that at her daughter-in-law's house she was served tea in a borrowed tea set because she and her son made their decision based on the fact that her now daughter-in-law came highly recommended after she had conducted a bit of *pooch taach*, a Hindi word that can be translated as "finding out." Most respondents admitted to finding out more about the prospective matches after the meeting by conducting *pooch taach*. This term is exclusively used to refer to a well-established practice for ensuring the credibility of a match by asking around the immediate community and mutual acquaintances or friends of the prospective matches about their backgrounds. It is something like requesting references from people whose judgment you value. It may not be possible to perform in all cases, but in most situations my respondents were able to establish a chain of acquaintance that resulted in a link to somebody who knew the prospective match and their family. For example, one's sister's friend who knew the prospective groom from college would be able to provide some impartial information on his "real character." While talking about this *pooch taach*, respondents would lower their voices and smile to indicate that it was supposedly a covert operation. Both sides ask relatives and friends about the other party's past and their background, all the while pretending to not know anything about this practice. Thus, it is after meeting the prospective match and conducting *pooch taach* and also following one's instincts that the decision to agree on a match is made. Nearly all respondents agreed upon the key role that instinct and intuition played when choosing the right person. On being asked what made them decide on a particular match, the answers would revolve around sentiments like "I liked the look of her" (Aman), "He reminded me of my father" (Noor), and "It just felt right" (Ash). This insight into the

role of emotions in deciding on a prospective spouse highlights the affective register of arranged marriage practices. I felt that my respondents were
involved in an ideal discursive presentation of what is expected of them in
the process of arranged marriage with some degree of self-awareness of the
performative nature of the process. This was reflected in the value they
placed on the minor slip-ups, or moments when the meeting would not go
according to plan, so that the mask of a perfect family would momentarily
fall, and one would be able to make one's decision based on the real person
and family.

Continuing Traditions as a Matter of Arrangement

A key concern among the respondents was continuing and preserving traditions. They discussed how the negotiation and performance of being seen
to follow the ritual of marriage arrangement was essential to their sense
of belonging to a wider British Indian community. To be seen as performing traditions and rituals such as the meeting works as currency that con-
firms their subscription to a community identity. The necessity for a sense
of community is heightened because of their status as a cultural minority
in Britain. More significantly, following the different traditions such as
the carefully choreographed meeting associated with the process of arranging a marriage was their way of re-creating an Indian home within Britain.
However, the invented and dynamic nature of traditions makes it difficult
to maintain any consistency in the practice of the rituals and customs of
arranging marriages. Hobsbawm and Ranger (1983, 4) argue that traditions
"are responses to novel situations which take the form of reference to old
situations, or which establish their own past by quasi-obligatory repeti-
tion." And it is here that the influence of global media in determining the
traditions surrounding arranged marriages is particularly interesting. For
a narrative of what the traditions were and how they could be practiced,
many respondents relied on global media exports such as Bollywood
films. Dwyer (2004) and Uberoi (1998) have argued that Bollywood films
portray an idealistic version of Indian femininity and the institution of
arranged marriages. Hindi romantic comedies are popular among the
majority of British Indians. They typically center on the theme of love and
marriage. The rituals and customs of marriages are scenarios around which

a number of hit Bollywood musical numbers are filmed. The representation of Indian culture in Bollywood crossover films made for the NRI market is emulated by South Asians, particularly the second generation, in their observance of particular customs and rituals. As Mr. Shukla, who had organized a Bollywood-themed wedding for his daughter, explains, "You see we don't have the good fortune of having our traditions passed on to the younger generation by grandmothers and aunties as you would in India. We are a small community, most of my extended family, my elders as it were, are back in India . . . so how do we teach our children what our rituals and customs are? . . . My daughter loves Hindi movies, the little Hindi she speaks is picked up from Bollywood films and in the process she also learns about what Indian culture is. . . . I know it's not always the real thing but at least it is better than nothing."

For Mr. Shukla, Bollywood films, with their representation of Indian culture, become an easy way of passing on some version of Indian culture to his daughters. He points out that in the absence of his extended family, particularly those of the elderly female members of the family, he has to rely on Hindi films as a source of sharing his Indian heritage. The fact that he admits that the way Indian family life and culture are portrayed in Hindi films is "not always the real thing" is worth noting. I would argue that with traditions there is no real thing; their practice is nearly always invented and fabricated from the resources of memory. However, for Mr. Shukla arranged marriage traditions and their practice would be more real and authentic only if they took place in India. He believes that there exists a real Indian culture, one that is back home, and that as migrants they have to rely on popular media representations to pass it on to future generations. This sentiment, that there is a proper way to follow traditions and that as migrants they can hope only to replicate some features of these traditions with the help of modern means of media and communication, was shared by many of my respondents. Following a Hindi film version of some of the traditions associated with arranged marriages works particularly well. The popularity of the romantic comedy genre among British Indian ensures that both generations can share a common understanding of those traditions, so there is less room for differences of opinion in describing the performance of a particular ritual or custom. References to Indian films in describing the performance of customs and rituals help to create a shared intergenerational narrative of what a British Indian identity might entail, which helps in creating a sense of home away from home in Britain. Additionally, the process of arranging a marriage also featured different criteria for what made a desirable match in a man and a woman. I discuss these in the next chapter.

4

Becoming a "Suitable Boy" and a "Good Girl"

In the previous chapter I recounted the processes that are involved in arranging marriages among British Indians. I highlighted the highly ritualized nature of the process and the attachment the older generation had with the different traditions involved in the process and their strong desire to preserve and pass on these traditions to the next generation. The process of arranging a marriage always involves intergenerational interactions as the parents or older relatives and family members are expected to take the lead in the rituals while the people getting married are expected to follow them. It is vital to note that agreeing to follow the rituals of finding a spouse should not be confused with being forced into them—my respondents were keen to emphasize that the assumption is that if you have opted to have an arranged marriage you cannot avoid the traditions that come with it. While both generations involved in the arranged marriage process had a degree of self-awareness about the invented nature of these traditions, being seen to follow them was regarded as crucial to maintaining one's culture and more significantly one's membership among the wider British Indian community.

The arranged marriage process, as I showed in chapter 3, also invited a high degree of self-presentation from the participants as ideal candidates (future husband or wife)—the meeting the family ceremony in particular involved a fine-tuned and orchestrated performance by both families involved in the process. Indeed, the process of arranging marriages has a societal script—commonly followed rituals and practices (as discussed in the previous chapter) that each family participates in—but this script involves two sets of criteria for those getting married. One set of criteria is defined by the parents (of the prospective bride or groom) who take the lead in searching for a partner for their son or daughter, and the second set is defined by the man or woman having the arranged marriage, as encapsulated in their desires and wishes for qualities they would like to see in their future husband or wife. For the whole arranged marriage process to reach its eventual climax in a wedding involves finding a balance between these two sets of criteria such that both generations involved in the process are broadly satisfied with their choice. In this chapter I examine how this balance is achieved through compromise and negotiation between the two generations. I also highlight the gender differences that underlay these compromises. I argue that an intergenerational performance of the presentation of the self (Goffman 1959) underlays much of the arranged marriage process. The pressures to conform to idealized and conservative norms of femininity and masculinity were acutely felt by both the men and women getting married, although the pressure felt by women was higher. The second-generation respondents were able to negotiate around some of these norms by delicately employing soft-power tactics to change some of them while staying within the boundaries of overarching discourses that defined the codes of masculinity and femininity within British Indian families.

A Suitable Boy for a Good Girl

All my respondents referred to the one getting married as boy or girl rather than man or women, for two reasons. First, this is a result of direct translation from Hindi. When talking about arranged marriages, the search is referred to as looking for a boy or girl as in *ladka dekhna* or *ladki dekhna*, so even the respondents who spoke in English preferred to say "we are looking for a girl or a boy" rather than man or woman. Second, marriage is seen as a key rite of passage through which a boy becomes a man and a girl becomes a woman, and as such unmarried people are referred to as boy or girl well into their thirties. In this section I discuss how the different requirements for a husband or wife were discussed through reference to the notion of a suitable boy for a man and a good girl for a woman. I first discuss the parents' criteria as they take the lead in the search for an arranged match, followed by a discussion of the opinions and criteria of young men and women undergoing the arranged marriages.

A Suitable Boy

To borrow Vikram Seth's (1993) title of the same name to describe the ideal male candidate in arranged marriage seems fitting to me when nearly all the first-generation respondents used the term "suitable" to describe the type of man that they were seeking—"a man who would suit our daughter" or "somebody who would suit our family." The primary criterion that made a man suitable was good educational qualifications that translated into a stable, well-paying job. The male breadwinner ideal was central to the suitable boy criterion: "By good education, I don't mean one has to have a PhD [laughs] but a degree compatible with my daughter's. My daughter has an engineering degree so I would like her to marry someone with at least one degree, just A levels will not do." Mr. Singhvi, who expressed this desire, is a retired civil servant and was looking for a marriage partner for his daughter. Other respondents also talked about the fact that they had worked very hard to build a life as an immigrant and wanted the security of a good job for their daughter's partner:

> The first requirement is, has he got the right kind of educational background . . . because without education in this country we have suffered. We find that there is so much unemployment among members of ethnic minority communities. I also believe and I keep telling people we have to be five times better than the indigenous community otherwise you won't get a job. So that means, unless a boy has got a good educational background he would not be able to get a job . . . a good job . . . and if he hasn't got a job then he would not be able to look after my daughter. (Mr. Shukla)

For Mr. Shukla and Mr. Singhvi, an education preferably from a good university and a well-paying job were central to their requirements for a potential husband for their daughter. A sense of precariousness that comes with being a member of a minority ethnic population pervaded their expectations of who would make an ideal candidate as a husband for their daughter. The requirement for a good education was seen both in terms of status and as a guarantee for stability of employment. It also worked as a class marker where professional-class British Indians were keen to ensure that their daughter married into a class similar to their own. While the majority of the respondents stressed the requirement for a university degree as nonnegotiable, the importance that people attach to degrees was lamented by one Sikh father, Mr. Pandara, who told me that his son had been "rejected" by a number of girls because of his lack of a degree. "There is a lot of problem . . . the girl's family has their doubts . . . you see my son has a good business . . . but the girl's family is picky. He has done few courses like gym instructor course, car repair course that sort of thing . . . but people want degrees." The British Indians I spoke to appeared to subscribe very strongly to the notion that the man should be the main breadwinner, so a stable and well-paying job became the central criterion, along with the requirement for endogamy. It is important to note that this search for a suitable boy, when led by the parents, was part of a culling process whereby the short list of men who would be introduced at the meeting stage was determined by *the qualifying criteria* of university education and/or well-paying job and similarity in caste and/or ethnic background. Although the aim for the parents was always to make sure that they suggested potential matches within one's caste or above, most respondents admitted that they had become more flexible in this requirement, and increasingly small differences in caste were being ignored in favor of matching class and preferences for educational qualifications/jobs. The accommodations in caste differences were portrayed as a sign of changing times but also as the result of practical issues; with more and more marriages being arranged within British-born Indians, the pool of available caste distinctions is small. As Mr. Singhvi explained; "When people looked back home you had a bigger population to choose from, you could go to your home town and village to find people of similar caste, but now with the new generation, they don't want to marry somebody from India, and we don't have a lot of choice in terms of caste in Britain, so as long as they are Punjabi we are happy." In the Indian context, the preference for caste endogamy can be very specific, and fine-grained distinctions in subcastes and regional differences between them are accommodated in arranged marriages. However, I did not find this to be the case among the British Indians; for them, increasingly preferences for regional ethnic identity such as Gujarati, Punjabi, and Bengali of the prospective match had replaced caste preferences. The aim was to make sure that the potential husband or wife who was short-listed had a similar regional affiliation to India. Beyond the main criteria of a stable job and higher educational qualification, the other qualities that went into the makeup of a suitable boy were not stated in any detail. When I pushed my respondents to tell me more about what made a suitable boy, they would rattle off the familiar strain of "good education, good job," as Mrs. Nath explains; "Our job is to make sure that the person we find for our daughter has a good job, obviously they have to be educated. . . . Men offer stability, that is their primary job in marriage, the rest we don't care about that much, you know looks etc. They don't matter for men." This sentiment that men and their job offer a stable foundation for the prospective marital union was central to how the ideal male candidate for an arranged marriage was conceived. This is in keeping with studies on Indian masculinity that highlight how notions of Indian masculinity are intimately tied to the breadwinner ideal (Chopra, Osella, and Osella 2004). The parents saw this as their central criterion for a suitable boy when looking for a prospective husband for their daughter.

A Good Girl

In stark contrast to the rather limited requirements for men to be ideal candidates in arranged marriages, the criteria for women were much more exhaustive. The emphasis was on finding, as expressed in Hindi by my respondents, *Ek acchhi ladki*, translated as a good girl. The notion of a good girl figured prominently in my respondents' description of their choice for a desired match for their son. On being asked what constituted a good girl as a prospective match, the majority of my respondents (as I discuss below) listed a detailed set of attributes, ranging from very specific demands in terms of standardized norms of beauty to educational qualifications, "good character," family background, and a respect for and willingness to adapt to their way of life. Normative standards of female beauty were evoked by most respondents when discussing their criteria for a good girl. Consider the following quote by Mrs. Sharma. She came to Britain in the 1960s and works as a seamstress along with running a fabric shop. She has two sons, and for her a daughter-in-law should have the following qualities: "My son is really good-looking [laughs], no he really is, I am not saying it just because

I am his mother. So my future daughter-in-law has to be beautiful, fair, and tall, they have to match lookwise." According to Mrs. Lal, her prospective daughter-in-law should match her son "lookwise," an Indian English term used as shorthand for "in terms of looks or appearance." She wanted "a beautiful, fair and tall" daughter-in-law who would complement her son's apparent handsomeness. She also hastened to add that this was just not her view but her son had also expressed the same desire for a beautiful wife. She talked about how one of the *rishtas* she had received from a friend did not work because the girl had "a short haircut" and "her complexion was suppressed." Instead of saying she was dark-skinned, she declared that her complexion was suppressed and sheepishly noted that she saw nothing wrong with this but she would not match her son. This view that the prospective bride and groom's looks should complement each other was put forward by a number of respondents. The most common response was "they should look good together." Some respondents were aware of the fact that the demands they were making in terms of looks and skin color were not politically correct and might be seen as discriminatory by many, as the following comment by Mr. Shah highlights: "My son has specifically said he would like a pretty girl and there is nothing wrong with that . . . you know I have nothing against other girls. I mean look at you . . . you have a wheatish complexion and you wear glasses but I would say you are still a *sodi kudi* [nervous laughter]." Mr. Shah told me that in spite of my darker skin tone and the fact that I wear glasses, I was still a *sodi kudi*, a Punjabi term meaning a good girl. . . . He laughed while saying this to make light of the fact that he might have offended me. Skin color and tone as criteria for a match were brought up a number of times. The general preference always was for a fair-skinned girl. This was because the ideals of feminine beauty center on fair skin in India (Jha and Adelman 2009; Parameswaran and Cardoza 2009). Skin color was not seen as a consideration when it came to the prospective groom.

In addition to evoking conventional norms of beauty (defined primarily as fair-skinned, tall, and long-haired), educational qualifications were also regarded as an important consideration. For prospective brides, there were two ways in which people described their preferences: a highly educated professional who would match their son's academic qualifications or somebody who had a "mere BA" and was "more family orientated." In the case of the former, a highly educated professional always referred to a doctor, engineer, or lawyer. In the latter case, a graduate qualification, especially if it was in the arts, humanities, or social sciences, was seen as "merely a degree," with not much potential for a career. The respondents who wanted this match always stressed they did not prefer, as they termed it, a career-oriented girl. As Sangeeta argued, "They have their head too high up in the air," and she would prefer somebody who was "homely" and looked after their son. Sangeeta was in her early sixties and was active in the local temple committee. She was in the process of looking for a prospective wife for her son, who ran a real estate business. She said, "In the case of a girl it is a new life she is marrying into and if one is too educated and has wild ideas of one's own it makes it difficult to adjust. A homely girl always makes a good bride." This discourse of a "homely girl"—one who will "adjust easily into the man's family"—appeared several times in my conversations with parents and relatives when they described the ideal wife for their son. According to the *OED*, the word "homely" in British English translates as "plain or ordinary but pleasant" and is usually used to describe a place; in U.S. English it means "of plain appearance or unattractive" and is usually used to describe a person. However, in common Indian usage the term is used to refer to a girl or woman who is unambitious (in her career) and does not hold vocal opinions; the terms "simple" and "caring" were often used to describe the qualities of such a homely girl. The assumption driving the requirement for a homely girl was that a woman who was unambitious in her career (if she had a job) and was not very strong-willed would easily be integrated into the wife/mother/daughter-in-law role as envisaged for her by her husband and his family. Higher education and ambition were seen as interfering with this vision of the homely nature of a good girl; even respondents who stated a preference for a professional woman did state that they would prefer to find someone who "had a job but was still homely, you know a modern yet traditional-minded girl."

This notion of a modern yet traditional-minded girl came across as central to the making a good girl in the arranged marriage discourse. When I asked my respondents about how this contradiction in terms was achieved, I was told that in an arranged marriage context the term "modern" is translated as having a job and/or an education up to the university level and the term "traditional-minded" referred to a woman who would

follow the way of life of her husband and in-laws (the majority of British
Indians maintain joint-family households, where different generations live
under the same roof or in houses in the same neighborhood). Such an ideal
match was summed up by Mr. Kohli, who was looking to get his sons married when I met him:

> Ideal . . . well what I think . . . that the girl should be [pause] it is not
> only me who thinks this . . . but my son as well. . . . The elder one
> does . . . he says . . . well the girl should have a personality . . . she
> should have a career of her own . . . but [pause] . . . but she should
> be beautiful . . . there should be some attraction in her . . . she
> should be *chitti* [fair] . . . a kind of attraction that she should look
> beautiful without makeup. . . . He does not say she has to be fair or
> anything but that is what he wants. . . . And second thing he wants
> [pause] is that she should be accommodating of the family . . . follow
> our rituals, respect the elders you know . . . not try to change things
> too much.

For the majority of my respondents, the expectations for a future daughter-
in-law were primarily driven by the fact that since she would be moving
into their home and households, a woman who was accommodating or in
other words adapted easily to their lifestyle was central to the success of a
good match. The adaptiveness of the future daughter-in-law and wife was
described in terms of colloquial Indian English expressions such as "homely"
and "modern yet traditional-minded"—both were regarded a key characteristics for a good girl—the ideal candidate for a future wife.

More significantly, within these preferences were also woven expectations for what was described as a "good character." A good character was
one attribute that all participants wished for in a prospective daughter-in-
law. On being asked what constitutes a good character, my respondents
would often use terms such as "she should have a good reputation" and
"someone who is not too Westernized." As Mr. Juneja, whose two daughters
were happily married and whom he had brought up to have good character,
describes, "For girls it is very important to be not like the *goris* in this
country otherwise how will we be seen as Indians .You see most parents
give their children too much freedom, the girls (British Indian) that are
here. . . . I call them *black-gori* . . . they are even worse than the English . . . too

liberated, you never know when their downfall will occur . . . so this is the problem."

For Mr. Juneja, the term *gori*, "white girl," also refers to the supposed cultural practices that are prevalent among girls in the "West," "like drinking, smoking, sleeping around, not respecting their elders." As such, for him a woman who was like a *gori* does not have a good character. He used the term *black-gori*, black-white girl or woman. He and many other respondents used this term to describe an Indian woman who had given up traditional Indian attributes of femininity in favor of adopting Western cultural values. This definition of "a girl's good character" by extension also defined Indian culture and its values. This was imagined in contrast to British or Western values. So as another respondent, Mrs. Joshi, said, "*Goris* are too liberated, too modern, smoking, drinking, high rate of divorce and not respecting their elders." An Indian woman with a good character was somebody who was "modest, had respect for Indian culture, had never had a boyfriend and cared not just for herself but also the entire extended family." Black-gori is an interesting formulation, with the English term "black" employed with the Hindi/Urdu term *gori*. A kind of Occidentalism is at work here, driven (as I will show in chapter 6) by a lack of a sense of belonging to British society at large (exacerbated by experiences of racism and discrimination), which means that so-called undesirable traits in women are sublimated into the figure of the *black-gori*. A British Indian woman who had embraced Western habits of drinking, smoking, and sexual liberation was seen as not being a suitable candidate for an arranged match; presumably all such British Indian women would not choose to have an arranged marriage anyway. Here whiteness was employed in the context of representing all that is wrong with the West and with Western modernity at large. The construction of the "white West," seen as marked by a lack of sober characteristics such as respect for elders and regard for family and societal norms, was a trope employed by respondents to set themselves apart from the majority British population. Moreover, even though they were never mentioned openly, oblique references to conservative sexual norms such as a preference for virginity for the good girl in an arranged marriage were also often made when talking about good character. This was most often described to me as the requirement for the prospective daughter-in-law to not have been in a romantic relationship prior to the arranged marriage—as one of my respondents said, "Good Indian girls don't have boyfriends only husbands." Moreover, in my respondents' narratives, it was very clear that the demands being made in terms of a woman's character, appearance, and behavior were legitimized by citing a purist narrative of women embodying the essence of a family, a community, a society, and by extension a nation. This discourse of women and their character as being representative of a country's culture and values runs deep in Hindu mythology, where India is personified as a woman and referred to as "Mother India," and as such the women of the subcontinent are imagined as embodying the cultural values of an entire nation (Shetty 1995). This was seen as very significant and in need of preservation when one had left the shores of Mother India and lived in a foreign country. The idea that a bride would eventually become a mother and it would be her duty to transmit family values to the future generations was also evoked as a reason for the demands placed on the requirements for a prospective daughter-in-law.

As I have highlighted above, in contrast to the vagueness in the criteria for a suitable boy, most respondents were very specific regarding a good bride. Their stress on a "good character" and a "traditional-minded modern girl" for a prospective bride can be read in keeping with the long-standing feminist critique of gender relations in the subcontinent. Many studies (Sangri and Vaid 1993; Chaudhary 1994; Kapadia 1995; Jeffery and Jeffery 1996; Kakar 1998) have highlighted the patriarchal nature of some forms of Indian culture and the marginalization of women that is prevalent in many sections of Indian society and continues in practice among the British Indian diaspora. Since the parents (or older relatives in their absence) are entrusted with the opportunity to "short-list" suitable candidates for the person getting married, these views play a significant role in determining the social and moral codes that permeate the search for a marriage partner. While recognizing that patriarchal language and expectations were used frequently in these descriptions, as is evident from my discussion above, it would be premature to analyze these descriptions as just another symbol of the continuation of unequal gender relations within the British Indian diaspora. Instead, it is more productive to first understand the notions of suitable boy and good girl as necessary fictions. Following James Weeks's definition of gender, one could argue that suitable boy and good girl serve as floating signifiers and necessary fictions (Weeks

1995). They are both empty and overflowing with meaning—empty in that they do not refer to anything concrete but overflowing with meaning because they provide the templates through which arranged marriage negotiations are made and young people acutely feel the pressure to conform to these codes. The terms in their Hindi equivalents do not point to a concrete reality but function primarily as a vehicle for the older generation to codify their views on the different types of masculinity and femininity driving gender relations in an arranged marriage context. Second, it is also important to appreciate the prospective nature of these signifiers; it was clear that the terms were used to describe the ideal qualities of a future daughter- or son-in-law who were conceived as a composite of hegemonic masculine and idealized feminine attributes prevalent primarily among first-generation British Indians with the knowledge that they will form only a template for the starting point of the search and that many negotiations will have to be made along the way. As Mr. Juneja describes, "You know there are no good girls and boys in reality, but we still have to try, it is a *tamanna* [hearty wish or aspiration] but you have to be ready to make compromises in the end." The fact that compromises have to be made was brought up often to counteract the apparent rigidity of the gender codes encapsulated in the narratives of a good girl and a suitable boy, where the respondents argued that while they may begin with some clear-cut notions of whom they are looking for, the eventual selection is a result of a negotiated choice between them and their offspring. As Zakir puts it, "Most people do manage to find a partner, even the so-called unsuitable ones . . . regardless of whether they fit the criteria of a beautiful, good-natured, highly educated professional that most Indian parents seem to be looking for [laughs]. You have to work on your parents." Working on one's parents referred to the delicate negotiations that the younger generation of British Indians made in order to steer the search for their future partner in the direction that they wanted, which I will discuss in the rest of this chapter.

Becoming a Suitable Boy and a Good Girl

You know when in school you filled in those teenage diaries listing your ideal man . . . he should be tall, he should make me laugh, he

should be kind . . . all that stuff. . . . Well . . . in an arranged marriage
when the time comes you do really have to think hard about what
kind of man you want to marry so that you and your parents can
then look for this person. And you know what? I found myself referring back to my silly teenage ideas, I just didn't know what I wanted,
like, you know more serious ideas about what kind of a husband
I wanted.

The above excerpt is from my interview with Kirti, a twenty-six-year-
old pharmacist who was in the early stages of an arranged marriage. She
had told her parents that "she was ready to get married now" and had asked
them to start the search for her future husband. When I asked her about
what kind of qualities she wanted in her future husband, she admitted to
not really having a clear notion of her future partner. Like her, the majority
of my respondents were equally vague about their criteria for a future
spouse. Raghav, a twenty-eight-year-old office worker, replied to my question about his aspirations for his future wife: "This is the most difficult
part, I don't know what I want most of the time, I can't even decide what
sandwich filling to get when faced with a choice so to know what I want in
a wife—no way [pauses] . . . hmm . . . I trust my parents."

The majority of my respondents claimed that they entered into an
arranged marriage without a definite idea of what they wanted in a future
wife or husband. In fact this was also the primary reason cited for why they
had chosen to have an arranged marriage. As Kirti describes, "If I knew
what I wanted I would have chanced it on a love marriage, arranged marriages are guaranteed to find you someone." The idea that love marriages
are for people who know what they want in a partner and arranged marriages are for those who don't was common among my respondents. The
focus on chance and guarantee is also illuminating as a key rationale for
arranged marriages. Many of my respondents mentioned how arranged
marriages were a way of escaping the tyranny of chance in love. For them
arranged marriages were an effective way of willing love to happen (I discuss this in more detail in the next chapter) with the person they and their
parents had chosen rather than leaving it to chance, as would happen in
a love marriage. In fact, they relied on arranged marriage as a cultural
resource that on the one hand allowed them to honor their parents' wishes

for continuing a sense of belonging to Indian culture within Britain (see chapter 6) while also giving them a definite chance of finding a partner. This was particularly true for the respondents who had semi-arranged marriages (see chapter 2) as they talked about how marriage was a significant rite of passage for them and they could not leave it to chance. Moreover, the feeling of security that came with having their parents involved in the process was also evoked as a reason for having an arranged marriage. Ranjan, a thirty-year-old engineer, said, "I trust my parents' judgment, which means that together we will make the right decision for my future."

I have gone into some detail at this juncture about the reasons my participants gave for justifying their choice to have an arranged marriage in order to highlight how their parents and their influence in the choice of a marriage partner loomed large in determining how young people rationalized their decision. Whether it was because of a feeling of security of a joint decision made in consultation with the elders in the family or the trust in their parents' judgments, the majority left the initial choice of selecting potential matches to their parents. The sense I got from my respondents, who either had had an arranged marriage or were in the processes of one, was, as Raghav said, "You let them have their right to start the search, see what they come up with and then you can start choosing." In such a scenario the floating signifiers of a suitable boy and a good girl adopted by the parents take on a new meaning as performative ideals of masculinity and femininity for the person getting married. The notion that if you were going to have an arranged marriage willingly then you could trust your parents to introduce you to suitable partners was common among the younger generation of my respondents. They were also aware of how their parents' choices and requirements were infused with conservative gender norms. All my second-generation respondents were aware of the existence of "the mythical good girl and suitable boy that all Indians families look for" and felt the pressure to conform to these ideals while also creatively negotiating the requirements to be a suitable boy and a good girl. I now turn to that.

For men undergoing an arranged marriage the pressure to confirm to "the breadwinner ideal" was acutely felt. It was very clear from my conversations with men that if they were unemployed the chances of a successful arranged marriage were very limited. Moreover, the pressure was felt not just in terms of having a job but also in having the right kind of job. As Rustum, a thirty-year-old graphic designer, explained, "My parents don't understand what I do so when it came to my marriage it was hard for them to explain to the girl's family that I had a good job, so I told them that they should emphasize that I work for a tech company." Another respondent who worked as a self-employed environmental consultant also talked about how he had to let his parents describe him as a scientist to make him a more desirable candidate in an arranged marriage: "Initially. I wasn't happy with this, it is not how I make a living, but it is also not a lie. I have a degree in environmental engineering so you could say I am a scientist of sorts." He described how he went along with his parents' description, but when it came to the actual meeting with the women his parents had selected for him, "it was really important to me that my marriage wasn't based on a lie, I told Malti [now his wife] the truth, described to her exactly what my job was and maybe that is why we are married as she liked my honesty." This was the most common negotiation men entering into an arranged marriage made; they let their parents modify their job description to fit with highly regarded norms among British Indians.

I also spoke with two men who were not employed at the time of the interview; they talked with despair about their lack of success in an arranged marriage. One of them remarked, "My mum keeps on saying we can talk about our family wealth but I don't want to get married without a job, I won't get any respect, the good girls won't have me." The pressure to have a job was also enhanced because of the strong association between masculinity and employment; nearly all respondents talked about how they would be regarded as less of a man if they did not have a desirable job. A young man who started his career as a waiter discussed how he toiled to get a promotion to restaurant manager in order to make himself a more desirable arranged marriage candidate. It appeared that there was a hierarchy of male employment within the arranged marriage setting, where professional jobs such as doctors, engineers, lawyers, and CEOs were at the top, followed by successful independent business owners and service jobs, with unemployment at the bottom. This political economy of marriage has been discussed by scholars (Sheel 2005; Kalpagam 2005) examining transnational marriages where the enhanced chances of social mobility offered due to migration translate to higher expectations of wealth and status from the woman's side of the family. I found that among the British Indians this was equally true of men who married among British-born women. Moreover, in addition to the pressure to have a so-called good job, some of my male respondents also reported feeling anxious about their personal appearance. Two of them had recently joined a local weight loss group as they felt that they had so far been unsuccessful in an arranged marriage due to being overweight. One said that he had been "rejected" by all the women his parents had introduced him to. A few also talked about worries regarding hair loss, but appearance for men did not come across as a major concern.

On the other hand, for the women conforming to standardized ideals of beauty was certainly a requirement. However, they negotiated this ideal in various ways; for some it was regarded as unwanted pressure to look a certain way and they resisted it, while others embraced it through a postfeminist rationale of choice and self-care (McRobbie 2009). For the latter group, beauty ideals were seen as something to aspire to, as Jaya said: "Well it is the most important meeting of your life, so you do have to make an effort, I grew out my hair, joined a gym, and even got my first facial." For Jaya and many other women, looking pretty in the conventional sense was not seen as a patriarchal demand, but they embraced the beauty norms associated with the discourses of a good girl and were happy to try to realize them through makeup routines and exercise. However, for the former group, the demands to dress and look presentable in a particular way were something to be resisted. Maya had been married for five months when I met her; she showed me her wedding album and asked if I noticed anything unusual in her photos. She was pointing to the fact that she was wearing spectacles at her wedding: "You know this was a small victory for me, us girls have to give up so much of our identity to look how people expect us to look, to wear glasses at my wedding was my way of saying that we don't always have to." She explained how she had always worn glasses and resisted the pressure from her parents to wear contact lenses to her wedding by negotiating an agreement where she wore them at the "meeting ceremonies" when she was introduced to prospective husbands but not at the actual wedding. Her reasoning for this was that she could tell the man she was meeting the truth and if he still liked her and they got to the marriage stage she would have the approval of her prospective husband to wear glasses. She indeed found this man (now her husband) among the several men she was introduced to and was proud of her small feminist victory.

My female respondents also pointed out that they encountered requirements of having a good character, as defined among British Indians in terms of modesty, and the formulation "homely girl" or "traditional-minded modern girl," which I have discussed in this chapter. Mrs. Keval, a woman in her thirties who had an arranged marriage, explained,

> It is unfortunate, I know that it is always a requirement for a girl to have a good character and not for a boy. . . . One's whole life is seen as leading to this point where this good character building will pay and we will be approached by a suitable boy. . . . As my mother used to tell me when I wanted to go clubbing like all my other university friends, that it is not our culture, we Indians don't do clubbing. This did not mean that I did not go, I would lie about staying over at a friends and would do all that students at university do [laughs] but I would not discuss this with my parents. My cousins did the same. So when somebody talks about this "good character" it is not something real it is just an appearance of having a good character . . . keeping up appearances is very important for us Indians.

The notion that the labor of keeping up appearances to preserve and maintain family honor and reputation was the primary responsibility of the women in the family was a burden that all my female respondents referred to in one way or another. The significance of honor and its mainte-nance among British Indians and other South Asians in general has been discussed at length in the literature (Werbner 2007; Grewal 2013; Mucina 2018), and I will not rehearse those debates here. However, I am interested in how the demand for a good character (understood as a sign of family honor) for a woman was met with reference to the notion of keeping up appearances. As Mrs. Keval mentioned, the performance of good charac-ter was more important than actively embracing the mostly patriarchal discourse that underlined the requirements of good character. While some of my female respondents admitted to lying to their parents about activi-ties that they knew they would not approve of, most had reached a com-promise with them, where the parents agreed to turn a blind eye to certain activities, such as going clubbing or drinking, if they were done in a discreet way and the women took up the freedom to do them but with appropriate considerations for their parents' sensibilities. None of my female respondents sought approval for these activities or tried to change their parents' opinions about what most felt were outdated views about women's character and honor. Instead, as long as the semblance of being a good girl was maintained, both the parents and the offspring were happy to go along pretending to not know about these so-called misdemeanors with the full knowledge of the performance that was being enacted. While this act of keeping up appearances seemed to mostly work for British Indian women as a begrudging compromise to maintain a reputation as a good girl in preparations for an arranged marriage, there were also nonnegotiable limits to what would be tolerated by parents, and in some cases compromise was not on offer.

For instance, Meena, who is in her early thirties and married as a result of an arranged marriage, talked about how in her late teens she became pregnant as a result of a relationship she described as "my school romance" and she could not convince her parents to let her keep the baby. Meena described her parents as very supportive and loving and talked about how, like other British Indian parents, they allowed her to lead "a Westernized lifestyle" as long as it was kept hidden from them and the appearance of a good girl was maintained. However, when it came to her pregnancy, she explained, "My mum straightaway said—we have to sort out this problem, have you told anyone else, no one should know, it will destroy our reputation." I asked Meena if she wanted to continue with the pregnancy. "To be honest, I wasn't sure, the boyfriend had dumped me and honestly I did not know what I would have done without my family's support, I did raise the possibility of adoption but my parents were adamant that was not an option and in the end it was terminated." For Meena's parents the importance of maintaining their daughter's chaste reputation took precedence over everything and there was no question of any compromise or negotiation with their hard-line position. Fearing that she would lose her family's support, Meena agreed to the termination. With her reputation of good character intact, Meena eventually had an arranged marriage and appeared to be happy in it. She did however tell me that she carries with herself not just the memories of the mental anguish of that event but more significantly the guilt and shame at having to keep it a secret from her husband. Meena's story is emblematic of what was left unsaid in many of my interviews when it came to describing the flexible nature of arranged marriages and the demands they placed on the men and women entering them. The majority of my respondents described arranged marriage negotiations as a playful jostling of power between the first and second generations; where small victories were won, some compromises were squeezed out in return for agreeing and appearing to follow the requirement of being a good girl and a suitable boy. The cost of these compromises, as Meena's story illustrates, was not the same for everyone; for some they certainly came with a high emotional and psychological expense.

In this chapter I have highlighted the key requirements that drive the performances of masculinity and femininity within an arranged marriage setting. Like the related concept of gender, the notions of suitable boy and good girl act as floating signifiers—as necessary fictions that determine the measure of the man or woman most desirable in an arranged marriage. While the pressure to conform to these ideal types was felt by both genders, the women felt it more intensely. I have shown how the practitioners of arranged marriages negotiate their way around the strict and patriarchal norms codified in these terms. They do this through soft power to eke out compromises with their parents and elders to make the arranged marriage setting work for them. Moreover, keeping up appearances for the sake of maintaining family honor and reputation was central to the compromises made by many women who had arranged marriages.

5

Learning to Love

This chapter focuses on the love stories of people who have an arranged marriage. It presents the different notions of love that influence arranged marriage. I theorize love as a set of competing discourses, meanings, and practices that shape our relationships with the "other." I show that contrary to popular conceptions of arranged marriage as a cold and calculating practice, considerations of love and romance form an important part of its exercise. Its practitioners distinguish between different forms of love and the accompanying obligations to individuals, family, and society at large. Although it is not regarded as the sole basis of marriage, love is nonetheless seen as a key ingredient in sustaining a marital union. This chapter illustrates the key idiom of love used by British Indians, such as in the conceptualizations of "love as a form of learning," to reveal the affective register of arranged marriage practices. The chapter is divided into two parts. The first makes a case for an epistemology of love by providing a genealogical exploration of how love has come to be understood within contemporary Western society. I argue for giving due eminence to the social, cultural, and linguistic arenas in which a certain complex of emotions and gestures is made intelligible as love to the self and the other. In the second part I examine two portraits of British Indian arranged marriages to show how love is understood as a form of learning.

What Is Love? The (Im)possibility of Researching Emotions

Asking *what is love?* is perhaps a fool's errand because of the sheer impossibility of representing the emotion for one and all. We may all have experienced love at some stage in our lives, and the uniqueness of that experience is partly why the idea of love is so powerful. In some ways we all already *know* what love is. For some love is a central tenet of the human experience, and there is no need to belittle it with academic inquiry. Indeed, much like with faith, we run the danger of losing it by putting it up to critical scrutiny and rational thought; ignorance can be bliss when it comes to love and its experience. However, as feminist scholars (Grosz 1994; hooks 2000; Ahmed 2014) have long argued, by relegating love and other emotions to the realm of the irrational we run the risk of ignoring the ways in which they are put in the service of politics and ideology. Moreover, by not recognizing the epistemic potential of emotions, we limit the horizons of academic inquiry by reinforcing "masculinist rationality" (Grosz 1994; Longhurst 1995, 98).

Alison Jaggar (1989), in her landmark work exploring the link between love and knowledge, offers us an outline of what an epistemology of emotions may look like. She argues that Western epistemology has traditionally favored reason over emotions. As such, emotions have long been either discounted from the epistemological terrain or neutralized in favor of a positivist approach to knowledge that regards them as biological facts and primordial responses to stimuli. Jaggar shows that even though the positivist view of emotions has now given way to more cognitive (or intentional) accounts of emotions (Nussbaum 2003), these approaches remain wedded to the artificial split between emotion and thought. In prioritizing the cognitive over the affective, cognitive approaches to emotions reinforce the traditional mind-over-body dualism of Western epistemology (Jaggar 1989, 156). Jaggar argues that emotions are best understood as socially constructed "active engagements" with the world that "presuppose language and a social order" (159). They have mental and physical, voluntary and involuntary aspects. For Jaggar, if we are to ever transcend the reason-versus-emotion dualism, we will need to rethink the relationship between knowledge and emotions by developing conceptual approaches that regard emotions and reason as mutually constitutive rather than contradictory.

More significantly, by emphasizing that emotions are epistemologically indispensable, she opens up a door for a critical theory that is self-reflective and pays attention to the attendant sociocultural field in which our knowledge-making exercise is played out. It is with Jaggar's blueprint for a more *sensitive* approach to knowledge making that I feel it is possible to ask and answer the question *what is love?* In this chapter I uncover one epistemology of love (among others) by exploring its interpretation in arranged marriage practices and more specifically ask how British Indians love in marriages where it is not seen as the basis of the marital union.

Romantic Love: A Partial Genealogy

Before discussing what love is for British Indians, it is important to explore the genealogy of the idea of love and its evolution over time. One of the earliest inquiries into the nature of love can be found in Plato's *Symposium*, where we find Socrates talking about philosophy as the love of wisdom. For him, love for the individual must be transcended for the love of the abstract, which means, for example, that the love for beauty in a person should take us toward the love of beauty itself as universal and divine. In doing so we may also be able to cultivate qualities (such as beauty, grace) in ourselves through the act of loving and eventually get closer to divinity. We could understand Socrates's approach to love as involving an education of our desires in pursuits of wisdom and beauty. This link between love and divinity can also be found in later religious discourses of the Bible and its commands for the love of God and virtue. Saint Augustine also reflected on the liberating potential of love as something that can lend us relief from desire and take us closer to God.

In the ancient world there was a strong recognition of the different types of love that can determine the relationship between two people (Offer 2006). For example, the ancient Greeks distinguished at least seven different love styles: eros (erotic love), ludus (noncommittal love), storge (a slowly maturing affection), pragma (a calculative quest), agape (altruistic love), mania (obsessive love), and philia (friendly love). All or some of these loves could go into the making of an emotional bond between people. It is noticeable that all these emotions still mark our experiences of love today, but we do not seem to distinguish them in such detail, and the word "love" appears to subsume all these different characteristics. More significantly, the love form that we recognize and value most in contemporary society— romantic love—does not actually appear on the horizon until the Middle Ages. The idea of romantic love is derived from the writings of Ovid's *Ars Amatoria* and has roots in the notion of courtly love in the eleventh century as exemplified in stories of knights and damsels in distress. According to the *Oxford English Dictionary*, the first use of the term was recorded circa 1650 when it was used as an adjective to indicate "having the nature or qualities of a romance [narrative work of fiction] as regards form or content." The first recorded usage of the term to refer to a love affair as in a romantic relationship between two people was found only in the late nineteenth century. It was first used as a term to indicate a relationship of romance between two people in 1844 and to refer to "love, esp. of an idealized or sentimental kind" in 1858. By this time romantic love had become a key theme in the new literary genre of the novel, and the travails of its pursuit are captured in the works of writers such as Walter Scott, Jane Austen, Stendhal, and Goethe. The success of Romanticism (1800–1850) as a movement in Europe was highly influential in popularizing the idea of romantic love (Armstrong 2002). With its emphasis on the emotional, experiential, and sublime over the rational, didactic, and realistic, Romanticism provided the perfect fuel for the ferment of ideas that celebrated the passionate, mysterious, irrational, and ecstatic nature of love, leading to what can be seen as the *invention* of romantic love. Once invented as such, romantic love turned out to be the foremost emotion of modernity, where its pursuit and realization into a companionate and loving marriage provided the foundation of individual identity, or to be more specific a *Western* modern identity.

Today romantic love is regarded as the most preeminent form of love, one whose invention, although traceable to a Western social history, appears to have an almost universal appeal. Romantic love doesn't exist only in Western societies but also features elsewhere, but making it the basis of marriage can be traced to a Western social and economic history. This romantic love and marriage complex is, in part, promoted and sustained through its constant cultural production in art, literature, music, and film. The growth in the mass appeal of romantic love in modern societies has been in parallel with the growth of the nuclear family, individualism, and consumerism (Giddens 1992; Beck and Beck-Gernsheim 1995). With the rise of capitalism and later neoliberalism as the prevailing wisdom of our times, romantic love has become the most sought-after and exaggerated expression of love. According to some authors (Kollontai cited in Jackson 1993b), the reason why romantic love has come to be the most decorated expression of love today is because of the extreme individualism that capitalism engenders, which results in creating an "inescapable loneliness" in the self, which we try to counteract by the pursuit of romantic love. Another interpretation for the modern preeminence of romantic love is that in a consumer economy romantic love represents "an economy or regard" of gifts and market exchange (Offer 2006, 308), where expressions of love are intimately tied up with our consumer selves. More significantly, romantic love and its pursuit has come to be intimately linked with the modern sense of self where self-identity is a "reflexive organised endeavour" and romantic love is a key ingredient in the "the reflexive project of self" (Giddens 1991). This identity project lends itself to a narrative presentation of self through the notion of the love story, thus making the search for and realization of romantic love a key goal of our lives. The relationship between romantic love and identity has also been explored by psychoanalytic approaches that emphasize the pursuit of romantic love as one driven by narcissism and self-love, where when in love we seek a version of ourselves (Kristeva 1987, 33). This narcissistic love is exemplified in the modern search for the perfectly matched partner, where compatibility becomes the precondition for love.

Whatever the reason for the dominance of romantic love in our emotional spheres, it is undeniable that it has become the new "fundamentalism" of modernity (Beck and Beck-Gernsheim 1995), replacing religion as the means through which we seek meaning and purpose. Romantic love as the key idiom of intimacy has far-reaching societal consequences, especially for women. Feminist analysis has shown that romantic love is crucial for our sense of self, but as an ideology it is also central to the sustenance of women's subordinate status in society. The key focus of feminist critiques of love has been to uncover the link between the "emotional and the material" (Jackson 1993a; Hochschild 2003). Feminist research has shown that emotional labor involved in being a wife, mother, and caregiver is linked to other forms of labor and the subsequent material exploitation of women reinforced by a politics marked by patriarchal heterosexual gender relations in the spaces of home and work (Millett 2000; Nagar et al. 2002; Mountz and Hyndman 2006). For some second-wave feminists (Greer 1971), the liberation from patriarchy and bourgeois marriage lay in unmasking the illusion of romantic love for a more liberatory version of love, one free from the expectations of heterosexuality and monogamy. Additionally, feminists have shown that there exists a "gender division of emotional work" (Duncombe and Marsden 1993) driven by a masculinist assumption that women are the keepers of emotions (particularly in household settings) and are more heavily invested in romantic love. This is because, as Diana Leonard (1980) has shown, the meaning of love is not the same for both the sexes; women have difficulty untangling sex from love. Thus, for women romantic love becomes the medium through which sexual activity is emotionally and to some extent morally validated. Consequently, love becomes a "means by which women in our society resolve the contradictions between being sexually desirous but not being sexually experienced. They sublimate their sexual feeling into a 'courtly love mould' and thereby ignore the passive, dominated role they must occupy in heterosexual courtship" (Leonard 1980, 262). This feminist analysis of romantic love has been highly influential in highlighting the politics of intimacy in which emotions such as love function as regulatory constructs conscribing women to a narrow emotional and behavioral sphere.

This brief survey of the evolution of romantic love has highlighted the socially constructed nature of emotions such as love and their entanglement with ideologies such as family, patriarchy, heterosexuality, and capitalism. By tracing the development of the ways in which romantic love has come to predominate modern life we can see that love is not an ahistorical constant but a sociocultural construct (Jackson 1993a; Armstrong 2002; Lutz 1986) that cannot be said to exist as a meaningful experience outside of the cultural and social milieux in which it functions. Moreover, the expressions of love that are recognized and valued by us vary depending on the social and cultural regulatory regimes that condition our approach to love. In some ways love (and emotions more widely) can be seen to have two histories. One is the general history, as I have traced above, which follows the broad cultural changes in our society; but love also has an individual history, worked out in the life of each person who comes to love another, the history of how we as individuals negotiate and manage our affective attributes in the search of love. Thus, any attempt at tracing a genealogy of love will always be partial—partial as in *incomplete* as the individual histories of love take their own path, and partial as in *subjective* and stemming from a specific sociocultural standpoint. A critical epistemology of love will consider both; we cannot understand one without the other. The love stories in this chapter then are partial in both senses of the word. It is important to note that to say something is a sociocultural construct does not mean the same as saying that it is a mere convention or illusion that can be easily reconstructed or overcome through the creation of a new image; even critical feminist theorists will confess to falling for the affective pull of romantic love. What I mean here is that in conceptualizing love as a sociocultural construct we need to take a "weak ontological" (White 2000) view of emotions where their intersubjectivity, contingency, and indeterminacy are always taken into consideration in any accounts of self, other, and the world. In this book I take a "weak ontological" view of emotions that understands love as an epiphenomenal entity generated by human action in the act of loving, the significance of which can be partially grasped by language, music, art, and other cultural discourses, but its affectual attributes are unique and often nonrepresentational. We can use our social and cultural resources to recognize what it feels like to be in love, but when we do fall in love we are convinced that what we feel is something unique and different from all that has been described before. This uniqueness is perhaps where the magic of love lies. Arguing that the experience of love is socially constructed then is not to deny its affectual attributes but to try and make sense of them as they become our "active engagements" (Jaggar 1989) with the world. Additionally, it is fruitful to understand love not as a singular emotion but as a complex of concerns—a tying together of several emotions. As Armstrong (2002) argues, loving is not a singular endeavor; we are trying to do a whole range of things when we love and are subject to a range of *feelings* such as desire, lust, care, and fear, which are all intimately linked to our sense of self. Particularly in making love as the foundation of marriage or a long-term relationship, we are also engaged in "a basic judgment about ourselves and our place in our world, the projection of the values and ideals, structures and mythologies, according to which we live and through which we experience our lives" (Solomon 1993, 126).

The Politics of Intimacy in Love and Marriage

The thesis that romantic love is a Western invention, with Western societies viewed as the natural home of romantic love, has long been a well-established theme within academic literature. Moreover, since the eighteenth century, romantic love has also been established as a racialized emotion—one that contributed to the myth of European civilization as opposed to the "barbarism" of the nations being colonized (D'Aoust 2018; McGrath 2015). This thesis, for a while, had the unintended consequence of neglecting the study of love in non-Western parts of the world (Cole and Thomas 2009; Jamieson 2011). However, in the past twenty years anthropologists have recalibrated this assumption (Hirsch and Wardlow 2006; Jankowiak 2008) through rich ethnographic studies that show the different experiences of and expectations from love beyond its Western moorings (Rebhun 1999 in Brazil; Ahearn 2001 in Nepal; Wardlow 2006 in Papua New Guinea; Mody 2008 in India) and by examining how love and marriage intersect in a globalized world by highligting the affective dimensions of contemporary transnational processes such as cross-border marriages, mail-order brides, and economic migration (Constable 2003; Hirsch 2003; Brennan 2004; Faier 2007; Padilla et al. 2007; Patico 2009). This body of work has been instrumental in decentering the Western bias in conceptions of romantic love by highlighting both the universality and particularity of this emotion and its relationship with marriage. These studies approach romantic love as a fundamental human experience and a universal emotion (see, for example, Jankowiak 1995, whose research has found romantic love in 146 of 166 sampled cultures, and Padilla et al. 2007, who show global convergence toward a preference for what Hirsch and Wardlow 2006 have termed companionate marriage) while also uncovering the local distinctiveness of this emotion—how it is experienced and the relative value attached to it in relation to marriage in different parts of the world. My analysis also builds on this scholarship by showing how romantic love is valued within British Indian arranged marriages through an emphasis on "learning to love." Following Patico (2010), my concern has been less with proving the absence or presence of "real" or "false" love within arranged marriages but more with analyzing how British Indians pursue love and make meaning out of an institution that does not value it as the primary foundation of marriage. This becomes ever more significant when, as I argued in chapter 1, noncompanionate marriage forms have come under scrutiny due to the steadily rising hostility to immigration in countries such as the United Kingdom and United States. Indeed, arranged marriages, as practiced among minority ethnic populations such as British Indians, have long been regarded as a threat to British immigration control. Research has shown (D'Aoust 2018; Byrne 2015; Gedalof 2007) that there is an implicit suspicion built into British government policy documents with regard to arranged marriage because of a predominance of a normative idea of marriage where a "genuine or normal marriage" is seen as one based only on romantic love and nothing else. The notion that marriage has historically evolved as a sociolegal contract is obscured in British government approaches to arranged marriages (Yuval-Davis, Wemyss, and Cassidy 2018). The association between love and marriage is a recent feature of modern industrial societies; it is neither universal nor automatic. For most of human history, marriage was too important a matter to be left to the caprices of an emotion such as love. Stephanie Coontz (2006), in her book on the history of marriage, shows how love came to be the basis of marriage some two hundred years ago, at the same time as the rise of modern industrial societies in Europe and North America. Not surprisingly, the takeover of marriage by love also coincided with the Romantic movement in art and literature, where marriage came to be the basis and culmination of romantic love and its ideals. Scholars mostly agree (Macfarlane 1986; Giddens 1991; Povinelli 2006) that there is a strong correlation between the popularity of companionate or love marriage and the rise of capitalism. Friedrich Engels (1884/1902, 97–99; Macfarlane 1986) argues in *The Origin of the Family, Private Property and the State* that capitalist modes of production replaced "time hallowed custom and historical right by purchase and sale, by 'free contract.' In order to make valid contracts people had to be seen as being 'free' and 'equal' and the creation of these 'free' and 'equal' people was precisely the main functions of capitalist production." Since marriage was a sociolegal contract (although not always entered into by free will) it also had to be recast as a contract entered into by "free" and "equal" individuals, so although "marriage remained class marriage . . . a certain degree of choice was accorded to the contracting parties." The choice was based on the precondition of the existence of romantic love or sexlove, as he calls it, between the contracting parties and "the love match was proclaimed as a human right" (Engels

1884/1902, 98) not just for men but for women too. Engels notes that the irony in this case was that although most other rights remained the privilege of the ruling classes and were curtailed for the proletarians; with no property or private capital interests to preserve, marriages based on love first became the norm among them and were taken up by the bourgeoisie much later. The historical-materialist answer for the shift from arranged marriages to love marriages then is attributed to the societal change brought about by capitalist modes of production and related values of individualism and consumerism. The freedom to marry whomever you wish is now seen as a fundamental right that any civilized, modern, and democratic nation should allow its citizen. More so than ever before marriage (and other long-term partnerships) rests on the elusive and unpredictable emotion of romantic love where individuals want "marriage to satisfy more of their psychological and social needs [and] to meet most of their needs for intimacy and affection and all their needs for sex" (Coontz 2006, 5). Romantic love has undoubtedly become the cornerstone of marriage-making practices in the West, but we would be wrong to regard it as a universal law. It emerged as a unique feature of European historical processes and was an evolutionary adaptation to a very specific set of circumstances.

As capitalism and neoliberalism spread across the world, non-Western societies have also slowly obliged to embrace romantic love as the basis on which a marital union should be contracted. In such a scenario, marriages that are not based on love, such as arranged marriages among people from the Indian subcontinent, are regarded as anachronisms that need to be updated to the more modern conception of marriage based on love. In migrant-receiving countries such as Britain and other parts of Europe and North America, its practitioners are viewed as people who have failed to integrate into the civic and social codes of their adopted countries. Moreover, the terms "arrangement" and "love" are held to be diametrically opposed to each other and help to foster a misconception that next to no notion of love features in arranged marriages and no arrangement is involved in so-called love marriages. As I have argued elsewhere (Pande 2014), the difference between arranged versus love marriage on a wider scale is seen as typifying the difference between the *traditional* Eastern and the *modern* Western cultures. Here, one can argue that a Western conception of the significance of romantic love in marriage (which in the West is also a recent phenomenon) is seen as the litmus test for how modern and liberal a culture is. While forced marriage has been made illegal in the United Kingdom and companionate marriages are seen and desired as the norm, arranged marriages end up occupying a gray zone between the two—always suspect and never desirable. As such, it becomes even more significant to question how we understand the emotional lives of migrants and diasporic community members, because as Mirza (2018) has argued, "History has repeatedly shown us that imagining a group of people as unloving beings serves as a prerequisite to mistreating them. While it is necessary for us to condemn violent and coercive social practices such as forced marriages, we must not malign an entire culture as the loveless 'other.'"

"O Tell Me the Truth about Love": Two Stories

The word love in English rolls off the tongue so easily, I love drinking tea, I love London and I love you, you speak Hindi don't you? Try translating these sentences. . . . It can't be done, at least I can't do it, can you . . . without making it sound trite and insincere? How can the same emotion be used to express my love for food and a person? Just doesn't work.

Here my participant Mrs. Pal is lamenting the overuse of the term "love" in English; she argued (when I asked her what love meant to her in her marriage) that the word for love in Hindi, *pyar*, doesn't work as a direct translation from English without losing its essence.[1] One could argue that this could be true for translation in general; direct translations rarely work in preserving the full meaning of the original. However, she was also pointing out the Indian reluctance to put one's feelings of romantic love into everyday speech. The majority of my participants said that they would never say "I love you" to their romantic partner in Hindi (they might in English, but it would be half-jokingly and would not have the same impact).

---

1. The quotation in the heading is from "O Tell Me the Truth about Love," in *Collected Poems* by W. H. Auden (1940).

The point that in everyday Hindi speech there is no equivalent to the English "I love you" is significant in distinguishing how my participants thought of love. They felt that it wasn't something one took lightly but a serious undertaking, one that determined the direction of one's life, family, and future children. It was also expressed between partners in different ways; some used elaborate expressions borrowed from Urdu poetry or expressions from films and literature, while others took pride in the fact that they have never felt the need to say it out loud to their partner. For them, their partner knows that they love them, and the power of the emotions is best preserved in letting it remain unsaid. In fact, the point isn't to say I love you but to show it in deeds and actions toward the other. My participants focused on how love in arranged marriage settings has *to be learned*. As I show through the love stories of the two couples that I discuss below, this learning involves two practices: first, it focuses on learning to love your partner; and second, it involves learning what Arundhati Roy has termed the "Love Laws—the laws that lay down who should be loved, and how. And how much" (Roy 2002, 33). These love laws are the tacit family expectations that drive one to find love within an arranged marriage setting based on commonality of religion, caste, and class. These laws are negotiable to a certain extent, with class and caste being more negotiable than religion (as discussed in chapter 4). The notion that love is something that has to be learned, whether learning what will be the acceptable forms of love within your family, learning to love the person whom you have an arranged marriage with, or relearning to love them again as you grow into the relationship, was a key notion uniting the love experiences in marriage among all my participants.

There was also a generational divide in this understanding where for the first generation learning to love involved educating yourself in loving your husband and wife; more specifically, the focus was that after the honeymoon period has ended one needs to remember to keep on learning about the person and relearning the ways in which one can love them for the longevity of the marriage. Needless to say, many people did not manage this learning, but the discourse of the British Indian concept of love and its function in a marriage was very much underlined by the stress on a normative approach to marriage and the necessity of love within it. Not getting married, among the people I interviewed, was still seen as "something we don't do." This then created two forms of pressures on the younger and second generation: the nearly universal and absolute social pressure to get married and the need to learn to love *the right person*, one who will fit with the expectation of the family and community at large. The second-generation British Indians argued how from very early on in their upbringing they began to learn the love laws of their family, which could involve a focus on endogamy of religion, class, and caste but even choices about the potential partner's food habits and career choices.

I highlight this generational divide in the learning of love through the stories of two couples that I discuss in the remainder of this chapter. The focus on love is intentional because, as I argued in the introduction, researching affective attributes of love and emotions involved conducting biographical interviewing techniques and was inspired by Michelle Rosaldo, who argues, "Feelings are not substances to be discovered in our blood, but social practices organised by stories, that we both enact and tell" (Rosaldo 1984, 143).

Mr. and Mrs. Pal's Story

Mrs. Pal subscribed to the view that you don't say I love you, you show it. I interviewed her with her husband, whom I will refer to as Mr. Pal, in their home on the outskirts of Newcastle. Mrs. Pal was a housewife, Mr. Pal a retired small business owner. They had been married for forty-five years. They were of an Indian Bengali background and still had family in Calcutta. They had two grown sons, both of whom also had an arranged marriage. I interviewed them in their home. Theirs was what Mr. Pal called a "traditional arranged marriage," which meant that he met his prospective bride only at their matchmaking party (as discussed in chapter 3) in the presence of both their family members. There was no opportunity to meet or date before the wedding. He mentioned how this was not the case anymore and that young people now have more opportunity to get to know each other before the wedding. I asked them if they had fallen in love when they agreed to get married and by the time of their wedding ceremony. They looked at each other and smiled, and Mrs. Pal ventured her opinion by saying, "I wouldn't say falling but yes we were planning to grow into love." Mr. Pal also nodded and said, "Yes I knew I was going to love her." This idea that you grow into love was common to how the other participants

I interviewed also talked about love in marriage. Here love was not imagined as an affectation that strikes you when you see somebody, such as "love at first sight," but something that you grow into; marriage provides the basis from which this growing into love happens. I asked them further, "But there must have been an attraction, otherwise how do you grow into love?" Mrs. Pal responded, "Attraction, yes I suppose I liked the look of him that's why I said yes to the match but it wasn't anything more, love came later." Mr. Pal joined in and said, "Yes thank God it did!" I dug deeper and asked if they could recall the moment when they learned that they were in love. There was silence for a moment, and then both said together, "After the tapes!" What had happened was that after the wedding Mr. Pal had to leave his bride back in India to go to England and get the necessary paperwork ready for her immigration. The other reason was also that his parents wanted to spend some time with their new daughter-in-law before she moved abroad to join Mr. Pal. This waiting period lasted some six months, during which Mr. Pal mailed his wife audiotapes with messages that he had recorded for her. He did this because he wrote joint letters to his parents and wife and felt he could not have any "romantic stuff" in those letters. Mrs. Pal remembered receiving the tapes very fondly. She talked about the moments when they "had their ups and downs" in the marriage, the tapes functioned like a talisman in rekindling her love for Mr. Pal and their life together. I asked if Mr. Pal wouldn't mind telling me what he said in the tapes. "They were just my musings, I used to record them at the end of the day, say what I did during the day and sometimes I would read a poem." "One you had written?" I asked. "No just from literature, Ghalib you know."[2] He went on to reveal that the process of making those tapes and sending them to India was a defining moment in their relationship because through the tapes he wasn't just passing on mundane details of his life in England but was also involved in wooing her, "showing her that he was creating a space for her" in his life and future. Mr. and Mrs. Pal represent for me one of those rarest of things—a happy marriage that has stood the test of time. Their story also captures their sanguine approach to the caprices of love. They claimed to be traditional people who believed in the Indian dictum

---

2. Ghalib was an Urdu and Persian poet writing during the first half of the nineteenth century in India.

that you fall in love with your husband or wife within a marriage and that loving a person inside and not outside of marriage was part of the Indian and British Indian approach to love. There was also focus here on appreciating what the Greeks referred to as storge—a slowly maturing affection for the other that can involve friendship, romance, and sexual relations as different arrangements of love for sustaining a relationship.

Kanta and Alok's Story

Kanta and Alok's love story involved learning to love the right person. Kanta was a second-generation British Indian, while Alok was from the Punjab. They were both in their mid-thirties. Alok worked as an orthopedic surgeon and met Kanta at a friend's wedding in London. He had been in the United Kingdom to advance his professional training. I interviewed them together. They told me how theirs was not a traditional arranged marriage. Kanta talked about how she arranged to fall in love with the right person. In the spectrum of arranged marriage practices, their marriage falls under the category of love-cum-arranged marriage (see chapter 2 for details). She had learned the love laws of her family such as what her boundaries were, especially in terms of whom she could go out with. She described how she was lucky that she fell in love with a Hindu Punjabi boy, otherwise things would have been very difficult. She also explained that her mother was a single parent bringing up three daughters on her own in a foreign country, so it was important for Kanta as the eldest child to set an example for her younger siblings. Kanta and Alok both appeared to have a very definite idea of the importance of the decision to get married and how it would determine their future lives. They both used the term "institution" when they referred to marriage. They repeatedly talked about how they had rationally thought about the decision to get married and that though they had fallen in love it was not based on an impulse.

ALOK: Well you see Raksha . . . marriage is not a joke. . . . It is not something we take lightly . . . especially in our culture . . . it is for life and so. . . .

KANTA: Well for seven lives according to Hinduism [laughs].

ALOK: Yes [laughs] not only for life but after life as well. . . . So personally for me I wasn't in a hurry neither to fall in love nor to get married. I was doing well in my job had a good circle of friends so there wasn't anything lacking. . . . I did have a plan though that I would not hurry into getting married. . . . All that love at first sight sort of thing isn't for us.

KANTA: And then you met me. . . .

ALOK: Yes, and then I met Kanta, she was smart, pretty, the kind of person I thought I could spend my life with . . . who would fit with my family.

ALOK: Yes . . . it sounds strange but we did weigh the pros and cons of this arrangement . . . see marriage is an arrangement, whether you fall in love or not. I had to see whether the institution of marriage was going to work for me in that period in my life and I reasoned to myself yes it would . . . that I wanted a life partner and that it was going to be Kanta.

KANTA: Yeah I must say I wasn't that rational, girls think differently . . . don't they. . . . But yeah he did fit the bill, he was from our culture, he had a good job, he seemed the sort of guy who would take care of me. I was lucky I fell in love with the right person.

In Kanta and Alok's narrative we find that the idea of Western-style romantic love, or love at first sight as Alok puts it, as a basis of marriage was not seen as very socially productive especially for a migrant and minority Asian population. The need for romance however was incorporated in the arrangement, albeit only as a secondary consideration. This was achieved by falling in love "with the right person," one who would satisfy and match the family's criteria of class, caste, religiosity, educational background, and preferences for physical appearance. Kanta and Alok have an interesting take on the nature of romantic love, where the incidental and predestined idea of finding a marriage partner was modified in favor of socially engineering the act of falling in love by arrangement, a common feature in love-cum-arranged marriages.

This emphasizes how for second-generation British Indians love as learning involved, first, discovering the boundaries of expectations and preferences of their parents and family in relation to their future marriage partner but second, and more significantly, putting that learning into practice by self-censure and falling in love with someone their parents would approve of. As Kanta and Alok exemplify, the deliberations involved in choosing a marriage partner were discussed in pragmatic terms of embracing a reflexive biography geared toward the creation of a good family life and subscription to a community identity. Since marriage was regarded as the only significant kinship tie that was entered by choice, its success could be ensured by successfully learning to love the right person not just for you but also for your family. For example, Kanta and Alok refer to how "in their culture" marriage is not a decision they take lightly. They argued that their individual agency was involved in their decision to get married and that there was also an element of chance as they had fallen in love with a person who fitted their parents' idea of their ideal spouse. Thus, the choices that they make are affected by the weight of tradition on one hand and a sense of relative freedom on the other. The idea of romantic love that involves an element of chance represents for Alok and Kanta the relative freedom that they have exercised in falling in love with the right person and not following the traditional method of short-listing possible partners with the help of one's parents or elders, as is the case in a traditional arranged marriage. They are able to convince themselves that they have complete control over the narrative of their biography, but it is not without the magic of chance, of romantic love or the lavish aspect of a grand Hindu wedding, or the social premium of being part of a community.

Learning to Love: The British Indian Way

I am tempted to compare the British Indian conceptualization of love to Friedrich Nietzsche's lyrical refrain that "Love, too as to be learned." In aphorism 334 in *The Gay Science* he suggests that like music "One must learn to love. . . . For there is no other way. Love, too, has to be learned." He points out that just as new music must be experienced for a while before we can learn to tolerate it, get used to it, and perhaps finally to love it, loving a person involves a similar process. For him love involves *learning the other* through the exertion of goodwill, patience, fair-mindedness, and gentleness. We find in the love story of Mr. and Mrs. Pal attributes such as patience and goodwill that drive their attempts at learning to love each other while enduring a separation immediately after the wedding when Mr. Pal left for England. Their notion of love in marriage involves getting used to the new partner and continuously learning and relearning to love your partner. This notion of love as a form of learning encapsulates a pragmatic approach to love, one where once you have accepted to marry a person you can train and educate yourself in loving them. Just as the first act of religious faith is the willingness to believe, in this conception of love what is needed first and foremost is a willingness and an openness to let yourself love and be loved by your husband or wife. Not surprisingly, most of my participants, who subscribed to this view of love, and—in the case of Mr. and Mrs. Pal—exemplified its practice, were first-generation British Indians who at the time I interviewed them had been married for over thirty years. However, a skeptical reader could discount Mr. and Mrs. Pal's story and say that it is easier to mythologize your love story when you have been with the same person for so long, and this focus on the pragmatics of love rather than on its enchantment is due to the mellowing down of the human spirit that comes upon some with advancing years.

Indeed, when I consider what form learning to love takes place among second-generation and younger British Indians, it appears that the focus on learning to love shifts to learning the norms of their family and carrying a burden of expectations of whom they should marry and how. Some like Kanta and Alok appear to internalize these norms and have found a happy balance between their and their parents' notions of love in marriage. They have achieved this primarily by narrowing down the arena in which they can love to correspond with the boundaries of religion, caste, and class set by their family. They have also successfully integrated the idiom of love within their arranged marriage setting by including courtship and dating between the period of their engagement and wedding ceremony. Kanta and Alok's story, although typifying many of the so-called modern arranged marriages among British Indians, was also accompanied by the silence (in my interviews) and frustrations of those who did not learn to love in this way. The absolute and uncompromising focus on heterosexuality in an arranged marriage setting did not leave any room for understanding love as a form of learning within same-sex couples. Moreover, the stories of people who could not or were not able to get married even through an arrangement (for a variety of reasons such as lack of family networks to facilitate an arrangement, lack of a mutual spark during introductions, or a general reluctance to take the plunge) represented a poignant reminder of the difficulty in fully embracing what could be regarded as an overly pragmatic and practical approach to love. What do you do when you simply cannot learn the codes of love sanctioned in your culture and want to break free of them? More significantly what happens in cases where after the wedding a seamless learning to love your marriage partner never happens? The unheard stories of these people provide a critique of the British Indian conceptualization of love as a form of learning but also highlight the challenges of making love and marriage mutually inclusive. Whether in a British Indian setting where love is strictly confined within the marriage setting or in the Western version where love becomes the basis of marriage/coupledom, no one is immune to the tyranny of the love-marriage complex of late modernity. So what could be interpreted as the emancipatory potential of love as a form of learning (which most significantly should allow the possibility of failure) is never fully realized in the British Indian idiom of love described above. My example of love in arranged marriages also shows how a tyranny of the romantic love complex functions in promoting a way of "being in the world" where romantic love is seen as the sole basis of marriage by privileging certain subjectivities over others and thus marginalizing other forms and practices of marriage and family.

The two love stories discussed in the chapter are illustrative of the most prominent idiom of love (learning to love) that I came across during my research. They illuminate the affective register of arranged marriages as opposed to their dominant stereotypes of a businesslike arrangement. My aim has also been to contrast the demotic and subjective negotiations in the practice of love with the dominant academic theses about the exclusivity of love-based marriages to Western modernity. As I have discussed above, the focus of much scholarly work on marriage and love has been based on a tacit assumption of the existence of "love marriages" as the means and signifier of modernity and social change, while the practice of arranged marriages has been relegated to the "waiting room of history" (Chakrabarty 2009). My research shows that arranged marriages are also sites of desires, affective anxieties, and individual choices; often the love stories in arranged marriage settings highlight the very personal negotiations that must be made when starting a new phase of life. They accommodate family interests but not at the cost of affective ties.

6

The Ties That Bind

Marriage, Belonging, and Identity

This chapter examines the arguments put forward by my participants as responses to my question, "Why do they practice arranged marriage in Britain?" The intention is to examine the views of British Indians on the utility, motivation, and most significantly the value of arranged marriage in their lives. It focuses on the views of the first generation (the views of the second generation are covered in chapter 4) because they were the main architects of a British Indian community ideal that furthered arranged marriage as a way of finding a spouse for the younger generations. I argue that the respondents' status as migrants and their consciousness of a migrant identity are central to the justifications and reasons they provide for the practice of arranged marriage.

Why Ask *Why*?

Before discussing the reasons why people practice arranged marriages, it is important to discuss *why* we should even ask this question. *Why* is this a cause for inquiry? Alternatively, why do I not ask why white British people do *not* have arranged marriages or why they have "love marriages"? One could answer this by evoking the spirit of sociological inquiry: I am interested in the concept of arranged marriages, I wish to know why people practice matchmaking to the degree that it is referred to as arrangement, and so on. However, the context, setting, and participants of this research make the answers more problematic than merely an innocent interest in the "other." Often the very fact that a culture becomes an object of scrutiny is because it is regarded as different and difference has to be acknowledged, researched, and even perhaps understood. This is reflected in early anthropological studies with their interest in non-Western cultures and the study of marriage systems under the concept of kinship (Radcliffe-Brown and Forde 2015 Karve 2005). As Lawler (2008, 36) argues, "Conventionally . . . the study of kinship in sociology . . . stemmed from an assumption that while non-westerners (the objects of study in traditional anthropology) had kinship, we (in the west) had families . . . and as such it was understood as a means through which non-western identities are forged."

The study of arranged marriage among Indians in Britain had also followed this spirit of inquiry where the anthropologist could stay at home in Britain and still study the exotic and the different (Telang 1967; Werbner 1986). I conducted my research with a group of people who trace their origins to the Indian subcontinent and whose migration to Britain is linked to the postcolonial condition. Their cultural practices that once formed part of the "culture of the east" are now at the heart of what was once the seat of an empire. The distinction between the core and periphery has been blurred by the act of migration. As such, a culture that could have been studied at a distance under the aegis of classical anthropology now has to be scrutinized in terms of its rightful or not-so-rightful place in British culture. The attributes of individualism, agency, and choice that have long been understood as markers of a Western modernity are, I argue, also the influences that British Asians are exposed to. Hence, an appreciation of the personal and subjective nature of the choice of a marriage partner in an arranged marriage warrants an approach that regards British Indians not as just migrants and representatives of their cultures in Britain but as parts of British society.

Consequently, an interest in cultural practices such as arranged marriage cannot be divorced from the politics of this research. The question I choose to ask, "Why have arranged marriages?," is not a mere search for the reasons behind the phenomenon but more a statement of my positionality and resulting social consciousness. I am aware of the pitfalls of formulating the question in the manner I did. For some of my participants, it insinuated that I was interested in finding out if they had a forced marriage or why theirs was not a love marriage. I was also conscious of coming across as judging the cultural practice. A reflexive recognition of the limitations and scope of this research question has led me to interrogate my motivation behind asking it in this particular formulation. So what do I want to portray by asking "Why an arranged marriage?" The answer to this is easier to contemplate in terms of what I do not wish to portray. I do this neither to achieve some sort of "normalising effect" by showing that the decision to have an arranged marriage is the same as the decision to have a "love marriage" nor to show how different the practice is. When I asked my respondents "Why have an arranged marriage?" I made sure that I clarified that I was not asking them "Why have an arranged marriage in contrast to a love marriage?" The aim is also not to speak for or in defense of the practice. My aim is to present the thought processes behind the decision to agree to an arranged marriage as they were discussed by the participants. I present a picture of the ways in which the respondents linked their sense of migrant identity to the practice of arranged marriage. The rationale is to destabilize the colonial imagery that constructs arranged marriage as "forced marriage" and projects its practitioners as not having any choice in whom they marry.

In order to discuss the various reasons behind the practice of arranged marriages, here I present vignettes from the lives of three participants. They are not to be regarded as presenting "the ideal type," but their views reflected the most recurring explanations provided for the practice of arranged marriage. A biographical account not only is necessary to provide a context for their arguments but is essential for analyzing and understanding the value that the continuation of the practice of arranged marriage brings to the lives of British Indians. As I show in this chapter, they reflected on their status as migrants in this country and discussed how their biography as an outsider in Britain was central to their justification of arranged marriage.

Preservation of Tradition: Dr. Shusheela Sharma

Dr. Sharma is a heart surgeon who works for the National Health Service. She came to Britain in the 1960s with two young children. She has been based in the North East since then. She has two sons, the elder one is married while the younger one is of "marriageable age." I came in contact with her when she was visiting the medical school at Newcastle University and had asked me for directions to the train station. She was keen to know about my research and invited me to her house for tea on a Sunday afternoon. On the day of the visit, over an elaborate spread of Indian sweets and snacks, Dr. Sharma discussed her views on arranged marriage. Her argument was that arranged marriage is a part of Indian culture. It is an ancient tradition and should be preserved at all costs. For her the practice of Indian traditions is what defined her as Indian.

DR. SHARMA: Well, we are a very traditional family. So, we wanted a traditional girl who would be following the way we have lived our life and been brought up rather than someone from here, who would be more Westernized in every way. Westernized in every way means language; most of the girls who are brought up here don't know our language, they have forgotten it a long time back, they don't dress in our Indian way they don't eat our food. I have no objection to eating Western food but as a regular thing just Western food and not Indian food. No. Westerners don't know much about our religion, they don't follow our religious ways,, so I can't see why we should forget everything we ever learned and become western. You'll never become British or wherever if you live outside your own country, you will never be able to become a person of that country, you'll always be a foreigner. If I am going to be a foreigner I prefer to be my own country foreigner rather than sort of half and half, you know, neither here nor there. . . . That's the reason why we prefer arranged marriage.

RAKSHA: But do you not think that your children grew up in Britain and as such would be more likely to follow British ways of life or perhaps they would negotiate with the way they chose to follow tradition.

DR. SHARMA: No why can't they grow up as Indians, just because they are living in a foreign country doesn't mean they can't grow up as Indians. Why can't they learn their language, why can't they learn their customs? Yes . . . well, that again depends on the way their parents bring them up. If the parents don't speak the language properly, if the parents don't teach them their religion and their customs they are not going to learn. As parents, preserving traditions is our duty by passing them on to the kids, otherwise we will be finished in this country, our identity will be lost.

Dr. Sharma regarded arranged marriage as a part of Indian culture, and living in Britain was very important for her to preserve it and pass it on to her children. She saw it as her motherly duty to bring her sons up as Indian. It will not come as a surprise to the reader that this view of preserving culture was common among nearly all the people I interviewed. Arranged marriage was regarded as embodying this culture and needed to be preserved. However, what makes Dr. Sharma's views interesting is in her own words the "personal journey of reflection" that had made her decide on this view of Indian culture. She talked about how her views might come across as very old-fashioned and dogmatic to many young people like me and that she had not always been like this;

> You know what Raksha, I was like you once, very Western, a female surgeon practising in Britain, it was big deal for an Indian woman in those days. I was by my choice of profession and education an epitome of progressive views. But as my children were growing up, I needed to give them boundaries, I did not want them to be hippy like and have them grow up all weird with no understanding of who they are. And I found myself falling back on what Indian culture had to offer. Now since we live in Britain, our cultural practices seem odd to them, they think that we are stuck in the Middle Ages mindlessly practicing ancient tradition which should have been changed and improved upon. . . . They don't think we are capable of choosing and reflecting on our cultural practices. For them the image of me wearing a sari and a bindi shouts out suppression and conservatism. . . . They think that if we had freedom [gestures the sign of quotation marks] we all would be like them and no one in their right mind would follow Indian culture.

Dr. Sharma makes a convincing argument for her insistence on preserving the tradition of Indian culture. She relates it to her identity as a foreigner in Britain and how she had made a conscious choice to follow her own culture and tradition. According to her, she was Western in many ways, by being a doctor, by being a single parent, by being divorced, and so on, but in the way she had chosen to live her life she was Indian, whether it was by wearing a sari or her insistence on continuing the tradition of arranged marriage. She employs some essentialized criterion to describe "Western" and "Indian culture." She uses the term "liberal" to describe her values when she was younger. She compares herself to me and says how she was "Western" like me once.

It is important to discuss why she makes this comparison. According to her, I come across as "being Western." She had been very intrigued by how I had managed to come all the way from India to a foreign country on my own and was doing research that involved a single girl like me going into strangers' homes and interviewing them. She had concluded that I must be somewhat of a rebel and pioneer among Indian women who could escape from the constraints that Indian culture puts on women. I explained to her that for me it had never been a case of rebelling against any cultural norms and that my parents were supportive of what I do. When I said that all my friends and classmates were also working or studying away from their parents' home and in many cases overseas, she did not seem convinced. For her the image of Indian culture and life was frozen in time as when she had left Calcutta to settle in Britain in the 1960s. This image of Indian culture, which she admits puts constrains on women, had crystallized in her imagination into a valuable tool to set standards for her children who were growing up in British society, where, according to her, there was too much freedom to do as one pleases. As a parent, she talks about the need to set up boundaries for kids, and these were available to her in the form of Indian cultural practices, such as arranged marriage, a very important part of this idea.

This view that migrants tend to develop a rosy view of their countries of origin and tend to observe traditions and rituals in a more strict manner than they would have done back home has been discussed in sociological and anthropological literature on migrant identity (Ballard 1990, 1994, 2001). Dr. Sharma's argument that she had a choice in bringing her children up with Indian or British values and that she chose the former demonstrates the impact this migrant imagery has on determining the ways in which she as an Indian interacts with British culture and society. Her imagination constructs the values, cultures, and traditions of her home country in opposition to the culture of Britain. The physical distance between the two countries also aids in developing an objective view of Indian culture and its superiority. This is because she does not have to deal with it in its entirety and can selectively choose particular aspects of Indian culture, which to a large extent are constructed from the reserves of her memory of what India was like when she left for Britain. And this imagination has helped her to visualize herself as an Indian or Hindu in Britain with some certitude because she can fall back on a set of guidelines that Indian culture entails. Consequently, arranged marriage becomes not only a way of finding a suitable match for her sons but also a manner of passing on her version of an Indian and Hindu sense of identity to her children and prospective grandchildren.

It is interesting to note how the respondents who talked about practicing arranged marriage to preserve an Indian view of life evoked the element of choice in their decision. They would nearly always discuss how as migrants they and their children had two cultures at their disposal and had had a choice in being part of one or the other. Needless to say, most of them had chosen the cultural practices of their place of origin. The arguments that they made to reach this decision varied a great deal. For some like Dr. Sharma, it was a question of how she wanted to bring up her children and her own sense of identity; she wanted me to understand that she had rationally argued herself into the choice of practicing and preserving Indian culture because that provided her with a familiar and comforting sense of place. She was also insistent in arguing that she did not think British culture was necessarily inferior, but it did not work for her as an Indian, who stood out as an outsider by her appearance and dress. She said how she will always be a foreigner in this country and she would rather "prefer to be my own country foreigner rather than sort of half and half." Not all respondents though talked about an element of choice between two cultures. Many, like Mr. Pandara, were convinced of the merits of their Sikh culture in contrast to "the lost culture of the West."

Arranged Marriage a Better Way of Choosing a Partner: Mr. Pandara

I met Mr. Pandara at a gurudwara, a Sikh temple. I was directed to speak to him by nearly all the other Sikh respondents I met there. I was told that he was the head of a Sikh residents' committee at the gurudwara and was a very active member of the Sikh community. Mr. Pandara was in his late sixties and married with two sons. Both the sons were in their mid-twenties, and he was looking to find a match for them. During the interview, he was insistent on convincing me about the superiority of Indian and Asian cultural practices, especially the merits of an arranged match. He argued how arranged marriage was a better way of choosing a partner and that even in Britain they used to practice this method but had lost it to "modern culture":

> If someone tries to take the mickey out of our culture . . . then I says to them well what are you saying . . . look at your Prince Charles he had an arranged marriage. . . . So we compare ourselves to royalty . . . we say to them you are low-class people. So you see there is a lack of confidence among our people.

For Mr. Pandara, practicing arranged marriage and other Asian traditions was representative of the older and better way of doing things. He justified this by saying how these were practices that were once prevalent in the West but had now been lost. He went on to argue for the superiority of the Indian way of doing things, especially the merits of arranged marriage:

MR. PANDARA: I'll tell you why we practice arranged marriage, I am a lawyer . . . right. . . . I will talk in terms of pros and cons . . . well no cons just pros otherwise I will lose the argument [laughs]. Arranged marriage is better because it matches things, class, caste, appearance, interests and we all know that it is easier to get along with people who share similar ideals to us.

RAKSHA: But what about when people say "opposites attract"?

MR. PANDARA: Oh that only happens in films, *kitaabi batei hai* [theoretical bookish talk] in practical terms and especially in marriage, you need to bring up kids, and if there is no similarity or maybe consensus is a better word . . . so if there is no consensus among the couples, how will you give the kids a stable base? You will be arguing all the time on what is right and wrong.

For Mr. Pandara, similarity in culture is the foundation of a good marriage. He uses the word "consensus" and argues that it can stem only from people sharing a similar cultural background. I pointed out to him that one can arrive at a consensus as a course of action without always sharing exactly similar views and that by arguing for similarity he was denying that even as Indians or Sikhs people may have different senses of what is Indian or

Sikh culture. In response to this he made some very interesting observations about Indian culture:

> You don't understand. We might be different, but that is the best thing about India. Did they not teach you in school that *Hindu, Muslim, Sikh Isai apas mai sab bhai bhai* [Hindus, Muslims, Sikhs, and Christians are all brothers]? We are Indian first and we think in an Indian way . . . an Eastern way . . . even the *goras* [whites] know that. They know how we are spiritually superior to them . . . that is why they all go to India to find themselves [laughs] . . . and what makes us spiritual it is our culture. . . . You see as I said before we lack confidence in showing off our culture . . . it is that old colonial inferiority complex. . . . We are better, our ways are better and anyways they expect us to behave in an Indian way and we should be proud of that. . . . I usually say in my speeches in the gurudwara that our ancient Indian ways are the best, we respect out elders we don't send them to old-age homes . . . we take care of them. Our women have modesty not like the *goris* . . . we have strong family values . . . and we should keep them like that. . . . What if they make fun of us? We'll show them we are better . . . anyways they expect us to be traditional and so I say to my congregation let's show them how traditional we can be and how good that is.

Mr. Pandara makes two observations here about the value of his version of Indian culture and its practice. There is no doubt in his mind that Indian culture is better than British culture and provides him with a better way of doing things. I could not help but notice how frequently he referred to the expectations of "they," which according to him referred not only to British people but also to what he referred to as "the West." He appeared to develop his sense of Indian cultural superiority on the basis that "they" know that we are spiritual, that we are traditional; and most interesting of all he goes on to say, "They expect us to be traditional." He argues how in reaction to the British expectations of Indian culture he encourages his congregation to "show it off." The idea of showing off a culture is interesting. In the performance of his version of Indian/Sikh culture, whether it is by practicing arranged marriage, dressing in traditional attire, or encouraging "modesty in women," Mr. Pandara is able to construct for himself a sense of Indian identity. This identity is not just a construction to preserve his culture but also a response to what British people expect him to be, an Indian, a Sikh, a bearer of a traditional and spiritual culture. In a reaction to the others' imagery of whom he is supposed to be, Mr. Pandara engages in essentializing his culture to an extent where it can provide some necessary friction to sustain a unique sense of being.

Here Spivak's concept of "strategic essentialism" comes to mind. Strategic essentialism emerged out of her critique of the Marxist historical collective called the Subaltern Studies Group. The concept of strategic essentialism is a "strategic use of positivist essentialism in a scrupulously visible political interest" (Spivak 1996, 214). In the case of Mr. Pandara and his congregation, one could argue that he is strategically applying essentialist notions of Indian culture to mobilize a representative identity device for his Sikh brethren. However, one of the most significant aspects of strategic essentialism is that it utilizes the idea of essence with a recognition and critique of the essentialist nature of the essence itself. This self-awareness of the limitations of basing one's culture on the flimsy foundation of essence was not apparent in Mr. Pandara's ideas on Indian culture and its practice. I argue that what is taking place here is a practice of what Homi Bhabha (1984, 128) refers to as "mimicry and mockery." In "Of Mimicry and Man: The Ambivalence of Colonial Discourse," Bhabha discussed how by encouraging the Indian middle classes to be trained in the English language and a Western education, the colonizers could have at their disposal an army of "mimic men." These were "of a class of interpreters between us and the millions whom we govern—a class of persons Indian in blood and colour but English in taste, in opinions, in morals and in intellect" (Macaulay's "minute," cited in Bhabha 1994, 124). However, Bhabha asserts that the ambivalence of colonial discourse is such that it not merely produced these subjects as mimicking English culture in the services of the empire but also encouraged them to destabilize the superiority of the colonial masters. To put it simply, these "mimic men" began to realize that if they were good enough to be able to become English in language, dress, and thought, then perhaps the colonizer's culture was not that great after all. Bhabha argues that with this realization came the confidence to launch a resistance against the colonial masters. However, in

their mimicking the colonial culture there was also an element of mockery. This entails that when a minority or subjugated culture forges an essentialized identity, it is in reaction to the majority's representation of their
culture. So when Mr. Pandara encourages his congregation to "show off"
their culture and says "they anyway . . . they expect us to be traditional
and so I say to my congregation let's show them how traditional we can be
and how good that is" he is engaging in mocking the majority's representation of his culture.

In his attempt to mimic what he thinks Westerners and British people
see as Indian culture he is also able to assert a level of self-confidence in
his rationale for "being Indian/Sikh in Britain." He can counter a sense of
colonial inferiority that his version of Indian/Sikh culture may encourage
by overdoing it, by showing it off to the best of his ability. This is also a
subversive attempt to "mock" the other's representation of his culture by
saying, "They expect us to be traditional and Indian or Sikh. We will show
you how well we can do it all by highlighting this version of our culture . . .
as timeless and spiritual and full of rituals and ancient practices." A very
self-aware performance of Indian and Sikh culture was apparent among the
congregation at the gurudwara. The following is an excerpt from my field
notes:

> Have just returned from the gurudwara at XYZ. The whole atmo-
> sphere there was very bizarre to say the least. . . . I can't put my fin-
> ger on it but it wasn't like a usual Sikh place of worship . . . which
> for me has always represented a sense of spiritual calm. The whole
> ambience at the prayer service was strained . . . not natural . . . nearly
> everybody was dressed in brightly colored Indian attire, all the
> ladies wore lots of gold jewelry and everyone seemed to make a big
> effort to look enthusiastic and happy . . . much like a born again
> Christian convention. . . . What are they trying to represent? No one
> in their native Punjab would go to the gurudwara dressed in all their
> finery.

I was baffled by this aggressive display of Indian and Sikh culture. It
also stood out more because the gurudwara stood in the compound of a
church. For the people I spoke to during the *langar*, the communal meal at
the gurudwara, this was a place where they could showcase their culture

and "be Indian/Sikh," and for some, like Mr. Pandara, "show off their cultural superiority." Thus, for people like him it was essential that their children follow in their footsteps to preserve this sense of identity based on an external performance of rituals and traditions, and an arranged match was thus very instrumental in achieving this goal.

Another trope that both Dr. Sharma and Mr. Pandara used in justifying their practice of arranging marriages was by invoking "the West" as a place characterized by a lack of spirituality and as having a culture marred by materialism. "The West" and by extension Britain, their adopted home, was described as a place that had lost its spiritual and moral compass. So Dr. Sharma discussed that she had a choice in bringing up her children between Indian and Western culture. She chose the former because she did not want them to grow up without any boundaries between right or wrong or like "hippies." Mr. Pandara defended the practice of arranged marriage by citing the spiritual superiority of his Sikh and Indian culture. They pointed out that arranged marriages were a better way of finding a spouse and building a family life because they provided a much-needed sense of spiritual order. The high rate of divorce in Western countries was cited as evidence of the adverse effects of too much individualism in the West, which for them was equated with being selfish. Thus, by setting up the West as an *other* they were able to situate themselves within the familiar discursive domains of arranged marriage and rationalize their reasons for continuing its practice.

Cultural Conflict and Its Problem: Mr. Aslam

One of the often-repeated reasons for why people had arranged marriages was that they were a better way of finding a partner than a love marriage. The argument would be that if one had a love marriage, in the absence of a similar religious and cultural background, a conflict of values and ideas would be inevitable and adversely affect the chances of a successful marriage. One of the respondents who was a strong proponent of this idea was Mr. Aslam, who ran a jewelry shop in the West End of Newcastle. He had lived in the United Kingdom for forty years. He was married to a white English woman and had six children—four daughters and two sons, five of whom were married. All had had an arranged marriage. When discussing the reasons for why he encouraged all his children to have an arranged marriage, he referred to the difference between the two cultures—i.e., his Indian and Muslim culture and the culture of Britain. According him the differences were irreconcilable:

> You see they are different I mean what the hell, their food is differ-
> ent, their clothes are different . . . they are two different lifestyles
> because one goes to church other goes to the mosque . . . one sits on a
> chair and the other sits cross-legged in the mosque . . . so there are
> differences you know one cannot reconcile those differences. It is not
> one meeting you know but every time. They have got their own tradi-
> tions and so that means every time there would be a conflict.

For him the differences between British and Indian cultures were so wide that a match between them would never work, or if it did it, the differences would always be there and one would always be reminded of them.

> See I tell you, when we go to our relative's place, yeah, we know
> how we are expected to behave we know we take off our shoes. We
> know who we are supposed to greet with a hug and who by just say-
> ing *salaam*. We know where we are supposed to sit in the drawing
> room, we know our culture. Now if it was a British person's house,
> I wouldn't know what to do, how to behave, I would stand out with
> my beard and *salwaar kameez* [traditional dress]. . . . I don't want
> that. I want to be able to fit it my daughter-in-law's house . . . not
> look like a misfit . . . and feel embarrassed . . . and it is the same for
> them as well. So why bring this upon oneself when one can marry
> among familiar people.

For Mr. Aslam, even trying to work at learning the ways of a new culture was not worth it when it came to marriage, as in his view one could
have an arranged marriage and save oneself the social embarrassment that
would come with trying to fit in. So while he talked about how difficult and
even futile it was to try to fit in with another culture, everything in his
biography suggested the opposite. He ran a successful business that involved
dealing with a foreign commercial culture and was married to an English
woman and so was not unfamiliar with adjusting to a new social life. When
I pointed this out him, especially the fact that he was married to an indig-
enous English person with whom I presumed he did not have an arranged
marriage, he presented me with the following argument:

[laughs] You see it wasn't a love marriage . . . it was arranged. . . .
I married her because I was an illegal . . . I had jumped ship you see . . .
but unlike my other friend who left their *gori* wives once they got the
passport . . . I did not . . . I have my honor. . . . I stood by her . . . she is
my wife for all intent and purpose. And she also gladly adopted Islamic
ways. . . . She is the mother of my children. You are right I have negotiated my way through this foreign culture, but I don't want my children
to do the same especially when it comes to family . . . what is the
point? We will never become them.

Mr. Aslam acknowledges that he has negotiated his way between
Indian and British culture, but when it comes to family life it is still better
to keep these negotiations to a minimum. For him the skills that he has
used to fit in British economic and social life by being married to a British
woman were not evidence of the fact that the two cultures might not be
that different and that differences may be reconciled. He argues that the
negotiations can involve a lot of effort and as such are not worth attempt-
ing if one can avoid them by having an arranged marriage with a person
from a similar cultural background. For him, the discourse of cultural difference works in two ways: first, it helps him to create an idea of Muslim
and Indian culture in terms of its difference with British culture; and second, once he has convinced himself of the existence of these differences
he uses them as a justification for why they cannot be reconciled and by
extension why these cultures are different. It is a classic circular argument
where the existence of cultural difference is based on the premise that the
supposed differences can never be reconciled.

What was quite interesting in Mr. Aslam's case was that his entire
family appeared to hold this view. I was invited to his grandson's birthday
party, where I got a chance to meet his extended family. As an outsider,
I could see what appeared to be a mixed gathering; there were relatives from
his wife's side of the family, his business colleagues, and his children and
friends. I was seated at a table with his elder daughter and her mother-in-
law. When I remarked that people seem to getting on well here and there
did not appear to be a cultural conflict, the mother-in-law retorted, "Oh
well! When it comes to food there never is a cultural conflict. . . . It is other
deeper things . . . like religion and what you do in the privacy of your house
that cause a problem."

This is a very telling comment on how my respondents engaged with and managed their own encounters with difference. A selective association with the "other," especially at the level of consumer culture, has been discussed by geographers such as Massey (1996) and May (1996). For Massey, a walk down Kilburn High Road with its myriad shops and displays of Indian, Bangladeshi, and Pakistani wares evokes a global sense of place. This implies a move toward a more progressive identity politics, one characterized by an appreciation in our biographies of the links and association with various cultures that make up a globalizing world. Scholars such as Paul Gilroy (2004, 15) argue for a *multicultural conviviality*, "the processes of cohabitation and interaction that have made multiculture an ordinary feature of social life in Britain's urban areas and in postcolonial cities elsewhere." Gilroy's convivial multiculturalism is thus evident in Britain in football matches, rap music, and British Asian Bhangra concerts, where people from disparate ethnicities and classes come together. Jon May, on the other hand, is suspicious of these claims. He argues that "race" and class play a role in determining to what extent and at what level we are willing to engage with the other. He discusses how for some white middle-class professionals an engagement with ethnic minorities may be in the aid of "a taste for the exotic" (1996, 206), while for some working-class residents of an inner-city London neighborhood an encounter with other cultures might lead to a reactionary sense of place expressed in sentiments of cultural conflict or even "racism" (1996). In neither case is a deeper engagement with the other evident, especially in terms of encouraging a progressive politics of place and identity.

The acceptance and admiration of a different culture is easily acquired at the level of consumer culture but does not translate into a wider acceptance through kinship and family relations. A global sense of place might encourage us to experiment with or even dabble in "exotic" food, dress, and music but rarely translates into a progressive identity politics. Conviviality is at the heart of consumer cultures of food and music. As such it is not surprising that people are willing to engage with cultures other than their own when it comes to sharing the exotic bounties of globalization as expressed in cultural exports of food or music. Our engagement with the other in the context of consumer culture as such thus does not express "the promise of a convivial multiculturalism but its limits" (Roberts 2006).

Hence, Mr. Aslam's mother-in-law remarked, "When it comes to food there never is a cultural conflict. . . . It is other deeper things . . . that cause a problem." One of the reasons why this is the case is that the sustenance of an ethnic identity is based on the premise of difference and the resulting practice of defining boundaries between us and them. As Appadurai (1996, 3) states, "The eclipse of the inherent negotiations and contestations renders ethnic identity a tidy cultural package, a template, with certain sets of meanings, behaviours, beliefs and boundaries—some are marked precisely because they highlight the boundary and others remained unmarked." In the context of arranged marriage, a desire to encourage your children to have an arranged marriage thus becomes a device to establish a boundary between home and foreign culture to distinguish between what is ours or *apana* and what is foreign or *paraya*. As I discussed in chapter 2, this *apana-paraya* distinction not only is crucial in understanding the significance of arranged marriages in the lives of its practitioners but also highlights the British Indian population's paradoxical sense of belonging to their adopted homeland of Britain. While on one hand arranged marriage acts as a boundary-making practice due to its focus on religious, caste, and class endogamy, on the other hand the modifications made to arranged marriage practices by incorporating elements of agency, romantic love, and choice also highlight its practitioners' desire to enact their own version of British Indian citizenship. The respondents' status as migrants and their consciousness of a migrant identity are central to this sense of belonging. The intertwining of marriage and migration discourses and the attendant politics of intimacy, which casts the practitioners of arranged marriages as illiberal citizens of modern Britain, serves only to reinforce this paradox. Consequently, this sense of belonging in between two cultures is manifested in several interrelated forms, such as through a desire to preserve traditions and cultures (Dr. Sharma) and to forge an ethnic identity based on difference from the mainstream (Mr. Pandara) while trying to create a space where cultural conflict is kept to a minimum (Mr. Aslam).

7

Conclusion

This book began by reviewing the existing frames for understanding arranged marriages as highlighted in the academic literature on British Indians. I discussed the problem of defining arranged marriages, especially when their meaning gets conflated with forced marriages. I also showed how arranged marriages occupy a gray zone between forced and love marriage. While the former has been made illegal in the United Kingdom and the latter is celebrated as a marker of a modern Western identity, arranged marriages become the object of suspicion and are increasingly subject to control and management by immigration regimes. This book thus makes an intervention in these debates by discussing the practice of arranged marriage from the point of view of its practitioners within the British Indian diaspora in order to understand the personal and affective negotiations that are involved in having an arranged marriage. As I am an Indian myself, at the heart of this book was analyzing the "othering" of my own practices and the reflexivity that follows from being "obliged" to speak for or to defend arranged marriages, which otherwise in a nondiasporic context would have been almost "second nature" for me. I have used a postcolonial theoretical framework to approach the *what, how,* and *why* of arranged marriages by looking at their practices among two generations of British Indians. In the context of *what* arranged marriages are, I have shown that there is no singular definition but a spectrum of matchmaking practices that are grouped under this umbrella term. I have made a case for approaching arranged marriage as a discursive practice, one that is employed by the British Indian diaspora to negotiate an ethnic identity by defining the boundaries between "us" and "them." More significantly, my respondents decided to practice their chosen version of arranged marriage in order to set into motion a narrative of reflexive modernity and citizenship. This is reflected in the practitioners' own discourse of the limits of "choice" and "arrangement" that arranged marriage offers them. For the first-generation respondents, the concern was to limit the influence of Western modernity (encapsulated in a move toward companionate/love marriages) because arranged marriage was seen as representing a sense of identity with links to the home country. This was reflected in the discourse of passing on and preserving one's culture. However, the second-generation respondents were more interested in navigating between the demands of their parents/elders and their individual preferences by creatively interpreting and redefining this traditional practice to suit their identities as Britons *and* as Indians. The "newer" forms of arranged marriages, discussed in this book, such as semi-arranged marriages, love-cum-arranged marriages, and, to a smaller extent, arranged weddings, all point to the negotiations made by the second generation in modifying traditional arranged marriage practices to suit their hyphenated identities. The book also provided an ethnographically informed interpretation of *how* marriages are arranged among South Asians in Britain. I described the role of various matchmaking channels used to look for a prospective spouse. The criteria employed in search of a match were analyzed under the discourses of a suitable boy and a good girl. The respondents' description and practice of the mechanics of matchmaking were driven by the need to be seen as keeping up appearances of following certain customs and rituals associated with the tradition of arranged marriages. I also highlighted the role of global media exports such as Bollywood films in determining the performance of these traditions. The reasons *why* people chose to continue the practice of arranged marriages in postcolonial Britain were closely linked to the respondents' strong identification with their status as migrants. In contrast to what my participants generally saw as the "incidental" nature of Western marriages, arranged marriages were favored because they were viewed as providing a sound and sober foundation for a sociolegal long-term contract like marriage. The considerations of matching class, caste, and religion were all regarded as the constituents of this foundation. The idea of romantic love as a basis of marriage was seen as not very socially productive, especially for a migrant and minority population. However, the need for romance was incorporated in the arrangement, albeit only as a secondary consideration. This was achieved by falling in love "with the right person," one who would satisfy and match the family's criteria of class, caste, religiosity, and educational background and preferences for physical appearance. This was an interesting take on the nature of romantic love, where the incidental and predestined idea of love was compromised in favor of socially engineering the act of *falling in love by arrangement.* Moreover, the emphasis was not on falling in love but on *learning to love*—this meant not only learning the social codes of your family and community that defined what boundaries had to be respected and which ones could be transgressed in the choice of partner through an arranged marriage but also learning to love the person you had chosen to marry after and within the marriage. The conception of love here was that of a slowly maturing attraction and emotional bond that would stand the test of time and act as a stable foundation for building a family and bringing up children. This meant that the deliberations involved in choosing a marriage partner were discussed in very pragmatic terms of embracing a reflexive biography geared toward the creation of a good family life and subscription to a community identity. Since marriage was regarded as the only significant kinship tie that was entered by choice, my respondents felt that its success could be ensured by creatively employing the practice of arranged marriage to find the best possible partner for life.

In conclusion, this book has sought to make four complementary claims to originality with respect to the extant literature on arranged marriages. These synthesize my core arguments around migrant identity, belonging, and arranged marriages. First, this book advances a postcolonial approach to arranged marriages by acknowledging the diversity and elasticity of the practices of arranged marriage. I have argued for an understanding of arranged marriage as a discursive practice as opposed to a timeless traditional custom. This approach helps one to appreciate the moments of cultural negotiations and reflexive engagements that are involved in this practice and their expression in the construction of a British Asian diasporic identity in postcolonial Britain. I have argued that there is no such thing as arranged marriage (singular)—only diverse practices grouped under this heading. I have highlighted the diversity of meanings and expectations that characterize the exercise of arranged marriages. I have also argued how by using terms such as "traditional," "modern," "arranged," and "choice," Indians in Britain are involved in value coding the discourse of this practice. That is to say, they use their own terminology to reflect on the significance of the arranged marriages in their lives. Whether it is a preference for the term "traditional" over "forced" or choices of family members over individual choice, they are engaged in mobilizing these terms to define the unique way in which they chose to practice arranged marriages. My empirical analysis of the various forms of arranged marriages highlights that there is a need to appreciate the elastic nature of this practice. Instead of making a simple causative link between a British Indian "culture" characterized by a tradition-bound society and a conception of arranged marriages as thwarting individual choice and agency, one needs to take into account the fluid and dynamic nature of such expressions. What I mean here is that if we recognize that the idea of culture is always in the making, a matter of becoming rather than being, then so is the practice of arranged marriage. My participants described the numerous means of looking for a spouse that contribute to a spectrum of loosely defined ways that can be dubbed as arranged marriages. None of the various types of arranged marriages on their own fully encapsulate what an arranged marriage is; rather, they signal toward what it can be depending on the factors that are described as being arranged. Therefore, by reconceptualizing arranged marriage outside of its dominant stereotypes, I have highlighted how the various discourses of arranged marriage are employed by British Indians to interpret and tailor this apparently traditional practice to suit their various individual and collective identity positions. Thus, I argue that arranged marriages will continue to have a place in British Indian cultural practices because they allow for the accommodation of shifting diasporic identifications with countries of origin and adoption.

Second, this book contributes toward the understanding of arranged marriage as one marked by a conscious exercise of the characteristics of modernity. This is in contrast to the popular conceptions of arranged marriages and its associations with the so-called traditional societies. My second-generation respondents in particular were keen to describe how they had chosen to exercise the very *modern* ideas of reflexivity, individual choice, and agency to opt for what is seen as a traditional practice of arranged marriage. This was done by creatively interpreting the questions of choice and arrangement with reference to the individual as well as the collective self. I have highlighted how the choice of a spouse was interpreted as varying between individual choice, parental influence in deciding on that choice, and the existential postmodern frustration of never having any free choice. In other words, my participants chose to incorporate the demands of modernity such as the ideas of romantic love and individual choice in their practice of arranged marriages. What this points to is a way of embracing modernity where the traditions of a past are intermeshed with the demands of the reality of the present. In the case of my respondents, this is manifested in a nostalgia for a past in terms of continuing the practice of arranged marriage but making it suit the realities of their present as residents in modern Britain. More interestingly, what came across was a narrative marked by aspirations for selective features of Western modernity. The approach toward adopting certain aspects of modernity was more in line with a desire for an identity that could be described as a progressive self. This was not just a result of a secular conception of self but also involved a reflection on the traditional, the spiritual, and the religious. The representation of this biography, one that tries to shoulder the modern and the traditional at the same time, was in aid of exhibiting a conscious attempt at integrating with British society and Western modernity at large.

Third, the popularity of arranged marriages as a means of finding a spouse is not simply a sign of a South Asian population tied to the customs and cultures of their countries of origin. Instead of being wedded to traditions, South Asians are skillful executors of arranged marriages who mobilize their culture as a tool kit in order to carve out identities such as British Indian and other diasporic forms of belonging. This is also the reason behind the popularity of the practice as it can be easily reinvented and reproduced with new inputs and interpretations by successive generations. The marriage patterns and traditions associated with arranged marriage are undergoing a reinvention. Moreover, all the forms of arranged marriages, whether traditional arranged marriage or an arranged wedding, are parts of an attempt at creating an identity. The operative words here are *creating* a British Indian identity and *enacting* citizenship. For some of my first-generation respondents, this could be achieved by popularizing the differences between "us" and "them," that is, by stressing the dichotomy of love and arranged marriage. For the second generation, there was an acknowledgment of establishing identities that pointed toward a more globalized and diasporic consciousness. As a result, the discourse of arranged marriage was underlined by a paradoxical sense of belonging that on the one hand involved preserving arranged marriage as a tradition to strictly observe the boundaries between us and them (because of the feeling of never being accepted by the mainstream and the experiences of racism and discrimination) but on the other hand also involved a conscious attempt at updating some marriage practices to a more modern ideal to enact a British Indian form of citizenship.

Last, I have also shown that gender relations within arranged marriages are marked by an imbalance in the expectations of performances of masculinity and femininity. There were many more demands placed on women to project a particular image as a suitable and desirable candidate for an arranged marriage. However, both men and women are expected to adhere to normative ideals of femininity and masculinity as defined through the discourse of Indian culture and the necessary fictions of a suitable boy and a good girl. Nonetheless, in spite of these demands my female respondents employed the customs and rituals of this practice to exercise their choices and aspirations for marriage. The process of searching for a suitable match and spreading the word is still a female domain. Mothers, grandmothers, aunts, and other female members of the family are the ones who take over responsibility for matchmaking. Here women are actively involved in the arrangement as it suits them and their wider family. Matchmaking and the choice of a life partner were regarded by my respondents as cultural practices based on the presentation of self, which among other things required an element of performance. So for British Indian women, succumbing to certain pressures such as pretending to know how to cook or wearing a sari for the wedding ceremony was seen as a small price to pay in favor of finding a compatible match. Some even actively negotiated the normative demands of femininity by seeking compromises from their parents and family members. Instead of an outright rejection of arranged marriages, my female respondents valued the institution of arranged marriage, with its numerous forms and flexible conventions, for the guarantee of family support and community identity that it provided.

Finally, I am aware that in making these claims I have prioritized the voices of respondents who actively embraced and chose to have an arranged marriage, and as such my research is marked by the silences of people who did not ascribe any value to the practice of arranged marriage or actively resisted it. These are people who did not confirm to the heterosexual basis of arranged marriages and/or those who actively resisted it. The stories of the latter have been captured in extant studies on forced marriages, but the former represent a glaring silence in studies of arranged marriages, including this book. I hope to address this omission in future research.

I close by arguing that there is a need to acknowledge the diversity of arranged marriage forms and their acceptance by British Indians despite the existence of hegemonic and culturally privileged forms of marriage representing "correct/modern" types of marriage. My key concern has been to unpack the modern expressions and lived experiences of arranged marriages. Thus, the empirical data in this research have taken into account a vast and rich array of everyday marriage narratives/trajectories and their interpretations among the South Asian diaspora in Britain. Finally, I propose that in order to genuinely appreciate the multiethnic nature of British society one needs to better understand the minority populations' own discourses of their cultures and traditions. Instead of using the yardstick of hegemonic norms to manage and control minority cultural practices, one needs to regard them as part of Britain, as another thread, among many, woven into the tapestry of the discourse of postcolonial British society. The associations of identity with nationality, ethnicity, religion, and culture are all imagined and as such can be *reimagined* in the context of a globalizing world.

REFERENCES

Abraham, M. (2005). Domestic violence and the Indian diaspora in the United States. *Indian Journal of Gender Studies*, 12(2–3), 427–451.

Ahearn, L. M. (2001). *Invitations to love: Literacy, love letters, and social change in Nepal.* Ann Arbor: University of Michigan Press.

Ahmad, F. (2001). Modern traditions? British Muslim women and academic achievement. *Gender and Education*, 13(2), 137–152.

—— (2006). The scandal of "arranged marriages" and the pathologisation of BrAsian families. In N. Ali, V. Kalra, and S. Sayyid (Eds.), *Postcolonial people: South Asians in Britain*. London: Hurst.

—— (2012). Graduating towards marriage? Attitudes towards marriage and relationships among university-educated British Muslim women. *Culture and Religion*, 13, 193–210.

Ahmed, S. (2000). *Strange encounters: Embodied others in post-coloniality.* London: Routledge.

—— (2014). *Cultural politics of emotion.* Edinburgh: Edinburgh University Press.

Alexander, C. (2002). Beyond black: Rethinking the colour/culture divide. *Ethnic and Racial Studies*, 25(4), 552–571.

Alibhai-Brown, Y (2019). Hidden torment of British men forced into arranged marriage. *Daily Mail*, January 19. https://www.dailymail.co.uk/news/article-6610763/Hidden-torment-British-MEN-forced-arranged-marriage-YASMIN-ALIBHAI-BROWN.html.

Anthias, F. (1998). Evaluating "diaspora": Beyond ethnicity? *Sociology*, 32(3), 557–580.

Appadurai, A. (1996). *Modernity at large.* Minneapolis: University of Minnesota Press.

Armstrong, J. (2002). *Conditions of love: The philosophy of intimacy.* London: Penguin.

Austen, J. (1816/2004). *Emma.* New York: Barnes & Noble.

Ballard, R. (1990). Migration and kinship: The differential effect of marriage rules on the process of Punjabi migration to Britain. In C. Clarke, C. Peach, and S. Vertovec (Eds.), *South Asians overseas: Contexts and communities.* Cambridge: Cambridge University Press.

—— (Ed.). (1994). *Desh Pardesh: The South Asian presence in Britain.* London: C. Hurst.

—— (2001). The impact of kinship on the economic dynamics of transnational networks. Economic and Social Research Council Transnational Communities Programme Working Paper WPTC-01-14.

Batabyal, A. (2001). On the likelihood of finding the right partner in an arranged marriage. *Journal of Socio-Economics*, 30, 273–280.

Batabyal, A., and Beladi, H. (2002). Arranged or love marriage? That is the question. *Applied Economics Letters*, 9, 893–897.

—— (2011). A stochastic dynamic programming approach to decision making in arranged marriages. *Applied Mathematics Letters*, 24, 2197–2200.

Baumann, G. (1996). *Contesting culture: Discourses of identity in multiethnic London.* Cambridge: Cambridge University Press.

Beck, U., and Beck-Gernsheim, E. (1995). *The normal chaos of love.* Cambridge: Polity.

Bhabha, H. (1984). Of mimicry and man: The ambivalence of colonial discourse. *October*, 28, 125–133.

—— (1994). *The location of culture.* London: Routledge.

Bhachu, P. (1985). *Twice migrants: East African Sikh settlers in Britain.* New York: Tavistock.

Bhopal, K. (2000). South Asian women in East London: The impact of education. *European Journal of Women's Studies*, 7, 35–52.

—— (2009). Identity, empathy and "otherness": Asian women, education and dowries in the UK. *Race Ethnicity and Education*, 12, 27–39.

—— (2011). "Education makes you have more say in the way your life goes": Indian women and arranged marriages in the United Kingdom. *British Journal of Sociology of Education*, 32, 431–447.

Biao, X. (2005). Gender, dowry and the migration system of Indian information technology professionals. *Indian Journal of Gender Studies*, 12(2–3), 357–380.

Blanchet, T. (2005). Bangladesh girls sold as wives in north India. *Indian Journal of Gender Studies*, 12(2–3), 305–334.

Blunt, A., and McEwan, C. (Eds.). (2002). *Postcolonial geographies.* London: Continuum.

Bonjour, S., and de Hart, B. (2013). A proper wife, a proper marriage: Constructions of "us" and "them" in Dutch family migration policy. *European Journal of Women's Studies*, 20, 61–76.

Bonnett, A. (1993). *Radicalism, anti-racism and representation.* London: Routledge.

Borneman, J. (1996). Until death do us part: marriage/death in anthropological discourse. *American Ethnologist*, 23(2), 215–235.

Brah, A. (1996). *Cartographies of diaspora: Contesting identities.* London: Routledge.

Brennan, D. (2004). *What's love got to do with it? Transnational desires and sex tourism in the Dominican Republic.* Durham, NC: Duke University Press.

Byrne, B. (2015). Rethinking intersectionality and whiteness at the borders of citizenship. *Sociological Research Online*, 20(3), 1–12.

Carby, H. V. (1982). White women listen! Black feminism and the boundaries of sisterhood. In Centre for Contemporary Cultural Studies, *The empire strikes back.* London: Routledge.

Casey, L. (2016). The Casey Review: A review into opportunity and integration. https://www.gov.uk/government/publications/the-casey-review-a-review-into-opportunity-and-integration.

Chakrabarti, T. K. (1974). Attitudes reflected in matrimonial advertisements. *Journal of Sociology*, 10, 142–143.

Chakrabarty, D. (2009). *Provincializing Europe: Postcolonial thought and historical difference.* Princeton, NJ: Princeton University Press.

Charsley, K. (2005a). Unhappy husbands: Masculinity and migration in transnational Pakistani marriages. *Journal of the Royal Anthropological Institute*, 11(1), 85–105.

—— (2005b). Vulnerable brides and transnational ghar damads: Gender, risk and "adjustment" among Pakistani marriage migrants to Britain. *Indian Journal of Gender Studies*, 12(2–3), 381–406.

—— (2007). Risk trust gender and transnational cousin marriage among British Pakistanis. *Ethnic and Racial Studies*, 30, 117–131.

—— (2012). *Transnational marriage: New perspectives from Europe and beyond.* London: Routledge.

Charsley, K., and Shaw, A. (2006). South Asian transnational marriages in comparative perspective. *Global Networks*, 6(4), 331–344.

Chaudhary, P. (1994). *The veiled women: Shifting gender equations in rural Haryana 1880–1990.* Delhi: Oxford University Press.

Chopra, R., Osella, C., and Osella, F. (2004). *South Asian masculinities: Context of change, sites of continuity.* Delhi: Women Unlimited.

Clifford, J. (1994). Diaspora. *Cultural Anthropology*, 9(3), 302–338.

Cohen, R. (1997). *Global diasporas: An introduction.* London: UCL Press.

Cole, J., and Thomas, L. M. (Eds.). (2009). *Love in Africa.* Chicago: University of Chicago Press.

Constable, N. (2003). *Romance on a global stage: Pen pals, virtual ethnography, and "mail order" marriages.* Berkeley: University of California Press.

—— (2005). *Cross-border marriages: Gender and mobility in transnational Asia.* Philadelphia: University of Pennsylvania Press.

Coontz, S. (2006). *Marriage, a history: How love conquered marriage.* London: Penguin.

D'Aoust, A. M. (2013). In the name of love: Marriage migration, governmentality, and technologies of love. *International Political Sociology*, 7(3), 258–274.

—— (2018). A moral economy of suspicion: Love and marriage migration management practices in the United Kingdom. *Environment and Planning D: Society and Space*, 36(1), 40–59.

Davidson, J., and Milligan, C. (2004). Embodying emotion, sensing space: Introducing emotional geographies. *Social and Cultural Geography*, 5(4), 523–532.

Del Rosario, T. C. (2005). Bridal diaspora: Migration and marriage among Filipino women. *Indian Journal of Gender Studies*, 12, 253–273.

De Munck, V. C. (1998). Lust, love and arranged marriages in Sri Lanka. In V. C. De Munck (Ed.), *Romantic love and sexual practices: Perspectives from the social sciences.* New York: Praeger.

Derrida, J. (1996). *Monolingualism of the other: or, The prosthesis of origin.* Stanford, CA: Stanford University Press.

Dirlik, A. (1994). The postcolonial aura: Third World criticism in the age of global capitalism. *Critical Inquiry*, 20(2), 328–356.

Donnan, H. (1998). *Marriage among Muslims: Preference and choice in northern Pakistan.* Delhi: Hindustan.

Donner, H. (2002). One's own marriage: Love marriages in a Calcutta neighbourhood. *South Asia Research,* 22(1), 79–94.

Dugar, S., Bhattacharya, H., Reiley, D., and Hall, M. (2008). Can't buy me love: A field experiment exploring the tradeoff between income and caste in the Indian matrimonial. Unpublished manuscript. http://www.aeaweb.org/annual_mtg_papers /2009/retrieve.php?pdfid=170.

Duncombe, J., and Marsden, D. (1993). Love and intimacy: The gender division of emotion and emotion work. *Sociology,* 27(2), 221–241.

Dwyer, R. (1994). Caste religion and sect in Gujarat: Followers of Vallabhacharya and Swaminarayan. In R. E. Ballard (Ed.), *Desh Pardesh: The South Asian presence in Britain.* London: C. Hurst.

—— (2004). Yeh shaadi nahin ho sakti! (This wedding cannot happen!). In G. W. Jones and Kamalini Ramdas (Eds.), *(Un)tying the knot: Ideal and reality in Asian marriage.* Singapore: Asia Research Institute, National University of Singapore.

Eade, J. (1990). Bangladeshi community organisation and leadership in Tower Hamlets, East London. In C. Clarke, C. Peach, and S. Vertovec (Eds.), *South Asians overseas: Contexts and communities.* Cambridge: Cambridge University Press.

Eisenstadt, S. N. (2005). Modernity in socio-historical perspective. In E. Ben-Rafael and Y. Sternberg (Eds.), *Comparing modernities: Pluralism versus homogeneity.* Leiden: Brill.

Ellis, P., and Khan, Z. (2002). The Kashmiri diaspora: Influences in Kashmir. In A. Nadje and K. Koser (Eds.), *New approaches to migration? Transnational communities and the transformation of home.* London: Routledge.

Engels, F. (1884/1902). *The origin of the family, private property, and the state* (E. Untermann, Trans.). Chicago: EH Kerr.

Faier, L. (2007). Filipina migrants in rural Japan and their professions of love. *American Ethnologist,* 34(1), 148–162.

Fink, J., and Holden, K. (2010). Paradoxes of gender and marital status in mid-twentieth century British welfare. In J. Fink and A. Lundqvist (Eds.), *Changing relations of welfare: Family, gender and migration in Britain and Scandinavia.* Aldershot: Ashgate.

Foucault, M. (1972). *The archaeology of knowledge.* London: Routledge.

—— (1980). Questions of geography. In C. Gordon (Ed.), *Michel Foucault: Power/ knowledge.* Brighton: Harvester.

—— (1999). *Madness and civilization: A history of insanity in the age of reason.* London: Routledge.

Fox, G. L. (1975). Love match and arranged marriage in a modernizing nation: Mate selection in Ankara, Turkey. *Journal of Marriage and the Family,* 37, 180–193.

Fuller, C., and Narasimhan, H. (2008). Companionate marriage in India: The changing marriage system in a middle-class Brahman subcaste. *Journal of the Royal Anthropological Institute,* 14, 736–754.

Gabb, J. (2008). *Researching intimacy in families.* Basingstoke: Palgrave Macmillan.

Gallo, E. (2005). Unorthodox sisters: Gender relations and generational change among Malayali migrants in Italy. *Indian Journal of Gender Studies*, 12(2–3), 217–251.

—— (2006). Italy is not a good place for men: Narratives of places, marriage and masculinity among Malayali migrants. *Global Networks*, 6, 357–372.

Gardner, K. (1993). Desh-Bidesh: Sylheti images of home and away. *Man*, 28(1), 1–15.

—— (2002). *Age, narrative and migration: The life course and life histories of Bengali elders in London.* Oxford: Berg.

—— (2006). The transnational work of kinship and caring: Bengali-British marriages in historical perspective. *Global Networks*, 6(4), 373–387.

Gardner, K., and Osella, F. (2003). Migration, modernity and social transformation in South Asia: An overview. *Contributions to Indian Sociology*, 37(1–2), 5–28.

Gedalof, I. (2007). Unhomely homes: Women, family and belonging in UK discourses of migration and asylum. *Journal of Ethnic and Migration Studies*, 33(1), 77–94.

Gell, S. M. S. (1994). Legality and ethnicity—Marriage among the South Asians of Bedford. *Critique of Anthropology*, 14(4), 355–392.

Giddens, A. (1991). *Modernity and self-identity: Self and society in the late modern age.* Stanford, CA: Stanford University Press.

—— (1992). *The transformation of intimacy.* Cambridge: Polity.

Gilroy, P. (1997). Diaspora and the detours of identity. In K. Woodward (Ed.), *Identity and difference.* London: Sage.

—— (2004). *After empire: Melancholia or convivial culture.* London: Routledge.

Goffman, E. (1959). *The presentation of self in everyday life.* New York: Doubleday.

Greer, G. (1971). *The female eunuch.* London: Macgibbon and Kee.

Grewal, I. (2013). Outsourcing patriarchy: Feminist encounters, transnational mediations and the crime of "honour killings." *International Feminist Journal of Politics*, 15(1), 1–19.

Grosz, E. A. (1994). *Volatile bodies: Toward a corporeal feminism.* Bloomington: Indiana University Press.

Gurak, D. (1987). Family formation and marital selectivity among Colombian and Dominican immigrants in New York City. *International Migration Review*, 21, 275–298.

Hall, R. A. (2002). When is a wife not a wife? Some observations on the immigration experiences of South Asian women in West Yorkshire. *Contemporary Politics*, 8, 55–68.

Hall, S. (1990). Cultural identity and diaspora. In J. Rutherford (Ed.), *Identity.* London: Lawrence and Wishart.

—— (1992). The West and the rest: Discourse and power. In H. Stuart and G. Bram (Eds.), *Formations of modernity.* London: Open University/Policy.

—— (1996). New ethnicities. In D. Morley and K.-H. Chen (Eds.), *Stuart Hall: Critical dialogues in cultural studies.* New York: Routledge.

Hirsch, J. (2003). *A courtship after marriage: Sexuality and love in Mexican transnational families.* Berkeley: University of California Press.

Hirsch, J. S., and Wardlow, H. (2006). *Modern loves: The anthropology of romantic courtship and companionate marriage.* Ann Arbor: University of Michigan Press.

Hobsbawm, E., and Ranger, T. (1983). *The invention of tradition.* Cambridge: Cambridge University Press.

Hochschild, A. R. (2003). *The managed heart: Commercialization of human feeling.* Berkeley: University of California Press.

Home Office. (2001). *Control of immigration statistics: United Kingdom 2001.* London: HMSO.

hooks, b. (2000). *All about love: New visions.* New York: William Morrow.

hooks, b., Steinem, G., Vaid, U., and Wolf, N. (1993). Let's get real about feminism: The backlash, the myths, the movement. *Ms,* 4(2), 34–43.

Isin, E. F., and Nielsen, G. M. (Eds.). (2013). *Acts of citizenship.* London: Zed Books.

Jackson, S. (1993a). Even sociologists fall in love: An exploration in the sociology of emotions. *Sociology,* 27(2), 201–220.

—— (1993b). Love and romance as objects of feminist knowledge. In M. Kennedy, C. Lubelska, and V. Walsh (Eds.), *Making connections: Women's studies, women's movements, women's lives.* New York: Taylor & Francis.

Jaggar, A. M. (1989). Love and knowledge: Emotion in feminist epistemology. *Inquiry,* 32(2), 151–176.

Jamieson, L. (2011). Intimacy as a concept: Explaining social change in the context of globalisation or another form of ethnocentricism? *Sociological Research Online,* 16(4), 15.

Jankowiak, W. R. (Ed.). (1995). *Romantic passion: A universal experience?* New York: Columbia University Press.

—— (Ed.). (2008). *Intimacies: Love and sex across cultures.* New York: Columbia University Press.

Jeffery, P. (1976). *Migrants and refugees: Muslim and Christian Pakistani families in Bristol.* Cambridge: Cambridge University Press.

Jeffery, P., and Jeffery, R. (1996). *Don't marry me to a ploughman! Women's everyday lives in rural north India.* Boulder, CO: Westview.

Jha, S., and Adelman, M. (2009). Looking for love in all the white places: A study of skin color preferences on Indian matrimonial and mate-seeking websites. *Studies in South Asian Film & Media,* 1(1), 65–83.

Jhutti, J. (1998). A study of changes in marriage practices among the Sikhs of Britain. PhD diss., Wolfson College, Oxford.

Kachru, B. B. (1983). *The Indianization of English: The English language in India.* Delhi: Oxford University Press.

Kakar, S. (1998). Feminine identity in India. In R. Ghadially (Ed.), *Women in Indian society.* New Delhi: Sage.

Kalpagam, U. (2005). "America Varan" marriages among Tamil Brahmans: Preferences, strategies and outcomes. *Indian Journal of Gender Studies,* 12(2–3), 189–215.

Kapadia, K. (1995). *Siva and her sisters: Gender, caste and class in rural South India.* Boulder, CO: Westview.

Karve, I. (2005). The kinship map of India. In P. Uberoi (Ed.), *Family, kinship and marriage in India.* New Delhi: Oxford University Press.

Khandelwal, M. (2009). Arranging love: Interrogating the vantage point in cross-border feminism. *Signs*, 34, 583–609.

Kibria, N. (2012). Transnational marriage and the Bangladeshi Muslim diaspora in Britain and the United States. *Culture and Religion*, 13, 227–240.

Korson, J. H. (1969). Student attitudes toward mate selection in a Muslim society: Pakistan. *Journal of Marriage and the Family*, 31, 153–165.

Kothari, U. (2008). Global peddlers and local networks: Migrant cosmopolitanisms. *Environment and Planning D: Society and Space*, 26, 500–516.10.1068/dcos2

Kristeva, J. (1987). *In the beginning was love: Psychoanalysis and faith*. New York: Columbia University Press.

Kuper, A. (2008). Changing the subject—About cousin marriage among other things. *Journal of the Royal Anthropological Institute*, 14, 717–735.

Lawler, S. (2008). *Identity: Sociological perspectives*. Cambridge: Polity.

Leach, E. R. (1961). Polyandry, inheritance and the definition of marriage. In E. R. Leach (Ed.), *Rethinking anthropology*. London: Athlone.

Leonard, D. (1980). *Sex and generation: A study of courtship and weddings*. London: Tavistock.

Levine, N. E. (2014). Marriage. In *Oxford bibliographies*. https://www.oxfordbibliographies.com/view/document/obo-9780199766567/obo-9780199766567-0016.xml.

Longhurst, R. (1995). Geography and the body. *Gender, Place and Culture*, 2(1), 97–105.

Lu, M. C. W. (2005). Commercially arranged marriage migration: Case studies of cross-border marriages in Taiwan. *Indian Journal of Gender Studies*, 12(2–3), 275–303.

Lutz, C. (1986). Emotion, thought, and estrangement: Emotion as a cultural category. *Cultural Anthropology*, 1(3), 287–309.

Macfarlane, A. J. (1986). Love and capitalism. *Cambridge Anthropology*, 11(2), 22–39.

Madood, T., Werbner, P., and Werbner, P. J. (Eds.). (1997). *The politics of multiculturalism in the new Europe: Racism, identity and community*. Basingstoke: Palgrave Macmillan.

Mand, K. (2005). Marriage and migration through the life course: experiences of widowhood, separation and divorce amongst transnational Sikh Women. *Indian Journal of Gender Studies*, 12(2–3), 407–425.

Massey, D. (1996). A global sense of place. In S. Daniels and R. Lee (Eds.), *Exploring human geography: A reader*. London: Arnold.

May, J. (1996). Globalisation and the politics of place: Place and identity in an inner London neighbourhood. *Transactions of the Institute of British Geographers*, 21(1), 194–215.

McFarlane, C. (2011). *Learning the city*. Oxford: Wiley-Blackwell.

McGrath, A. M. (2015). *Illicit love: Interracial sex and marriage in the United States and Australia*. Lincoln: University of Nebraska Press.

McRobbie, A. (2009). *The aftermath of feminism: Gender, culture and social change*. Thousand Oaks, CA: Sage.

Menski, W. (1999). South Asian women in Britain: Family integrity and the primary purpose rule. In R. Barot, H. Bradley, and S. Fenton (Eds.), *Ethnicity, gender and social change*. Basingstoke: Macmillan.

Millett, K. (2000). *Sexual politics*. Urbana: University of Illinois Press.

Mirza, F. (2018). Love in a time of migrants: On rethinking arranged marriages. *Aeon* .https://aeon.co/ideas/love-in-a-time-of-migrants-on-rethinking-arranged -marriages.

Mody, P. (2008). *The intimate state: Love, marriage and law in India*. New Delhi: Routledge.

Mohammad, R. (2015). Transnational shift: Marriage, home and belonging for British-Pakistani Muslim women. *Social & Cultural Geography*, 16, 593–614.

Mohanty, C. T. (1991). Under western eyes: Feminist scholarship and colonial discourses. In C. T. Mohanty et al. (Eds.), *Third world women and the politics of feminism*. Bloomington: Indiana University Press.

Mooney, N. (2006). Aspiration, reunification and gender transformation in Jat Sikh marriages from India to Canada. *Global Networks*, 6(4), 389–403.

Morrison, C. A. (2010). Heterosexuality and home: Intimacies of space and spaces of touch. *Emotion, Space and Society*, 5, 10–18.

Mountz, A., and Hyndman, J. (2006). Feminist approaches to the global intimate. *Women's Studies Quarterly*, 3(1/2), 446–463.

Mucina, M. K. (2018). Exploring the role of "honour" in son preference and daughter deficit within the Punjabi diaspora in Canada. *Canadian Journal of Development Studies / Revue canadienne d'études du développement*, 39(3), 426–442.

Mukhopadhyaya, M. (2012). Matchmakers and intermediation: Marriage in contemporary Kolkata. *Economic and Political Weekly*, 47(90). http://www.epw.in /system/files/pdf/2012_47/43/Matchmakers_and_Intermediation.pdf.

Myrdahl, E. M. (2010). Legislating love: Norwegian family reunification law as a racial project. *Social and Cultural Geography*, 11, 103–116.

Nagar, R., Lawson, V., McDowell, L., and Hanson, S. (2002). Locating globalization: Feminist (re)readings of the subjects and spaces of globalization. *Economic Geography*, 78(3), 257–284.

Nussbaum, M. C. (2003). *Upheavals of thought: The intelligence of emotions*. Cambridge: Cambridge University Press.

Offer, A. (2006). *The challenge of affluence*. Oxford: Oxford University Press.

Padilla, M. B., Hirsch, J. S., Munoz-Laboy, M., Sember, R. E., and Parker, R. G. (2007). *Love and globalization: Transformations of intimacy in the contemporary world*. Nashville: Vanderbilt University Press.

Palriwala, R., and Uberoi, P. (2005). Marriage and migration in Asia: Gender issues. *Indian Journal of Gender Studies*, 12(2–3), 5–29.

Pande, R. (2014). Geographies of marriage and migration: Arranged marriages and South Asians in Britain. *Geography Compass*, 8(2), 75–86.

—— (2015). "I arranged my own marriage": Arranged marriages and post-colonial feminism. *Gender, Place & Culture*, 22, 172–187.

Parameswaran, R., and Cardoza, K. (2009). Melanin on the margins: Advertising and the cultural politics of fair/light/white beauty in India. *Journalism & Communication Monographs*, 11(3), 213–274.

Parry, J. P. (2001). Ankalu's errant wife: Sex, marriage and industry in contemporary Chhattisgarh. *Modern Asian Studies*, 35, 783–820.

Patico, J. (2009). For love, money, or normalcy: Meanings of strategy and sentiment in the Russian-American matchmaking industry. *Ethnos*, 74(3), 307–330.

—— (2010). From modern loves to universal passions: Ethnographies of love, marriage, and globalization. *Identities: Global Studies in Culture and Power*, 17(4), 372–386.

Penn, R. (2011). Arranged marriages in Western Europe: Media representations and social reality. *Journal of Comparative Family Studies*, 42(5), 637–650. https://doi.org/10.3138/jcfs.42.5.637.

Phillips, A. (2007). *Multiculturalism without culture*. Princeton, NJ: Princeton University Press.

Pichler, P. (2011). Hybrid or in between cultures: Traditions of marriage in a group of British Bangladeshi girls. In J. Coates and P. Pichler (Eds.), *Language and gender: A reader*. London: Blackwell.

Povinelli, E. (2006). *The empire of love: Toward a theory of intimacy, genealogy and carnality*. Durham, NC: Duke University Press.

Puar, J. S. (1995). Resituating discourses of "whiteness" and "Asianness" in northern England. *Socialist Review*, 24, 21–53.

Puri, J. (1999). *Woman, body, desire in post-colonial India: Narratives of gender and sexuality*. New York: Routledge.

Qamar, M. (2017). *Trust no aunty*. New York: Simon & Schuster.

Radcliffe-Brown, A. R. (1940). On social structure. *Journal of the Royal Anthropological Institute of Great Britain and Ireland*, 70, 1–12.

Radcliffe-Brown, A. R., and Forde, D. (2015). *African systems of kinship and marriage*. London: Routledge.

Raj, S. R. (2003). *Where are you from? Middle-class migrants in the modern world*. Berkeley: University of California Press.

Rebhun, L. A. (1999). *The heart is unknown country: Love in the changing economy of northeast Brazil*. Stanford, CA: Stanford University Press.

Riviere, P. G. (1971). Marriage: A reassessment. In R. Needham (Ed.), *Rethinking kinship and marriage*. London: Tavistock.

Roberts, D. (2006). A world without race: Does black nationalism have to go too? *Boston Review*. http://bostonreview.net/BR31.1/roberts.php.

Robertson, R. (1992). *Globalisation*. London: Sage.

Rosaldo, M. (1984). Toward an anthropology of self and feeling. In R. A. Schweder and R. A. LeVine (Eds.), *Culture theory: Essays on mind, self, and emotion*. Cambridge: Cambridge University Press.

Rose, G. (1993). *Feminism and geography: The limits to geographical knowledge*. Cambridge: Polity.

Roy, A. (2002). *The god of small things*. Delhi: Penguin.

Rubin, G. (2009). The traffic in women: Notes on the "political economy" of sex. In R. Reiter (Ed.), *Toward an anthropology of women*. New York: Monthly Review Press.

Rushdie, S. (1980). *Midnight's children.* London: Penguin.

Said, E. (1984). Reflections on exile. *Granta,* 13, 157–172.

Sangri, K., and Vaid, S. (Eds.). (1993). *Recasting women: Essays in colonial history.* Delhi: Kali for Women.

Schmidt, G. (2011). Law and identity: Transnational arranged marriages and the boundaries of Danishness. *Journal of Ethnic and Migration Studies,* 37, 257–275.

Sen, S., Biswas, R., and Dhawan, N. (Eds.). (2011). *Intimate others: Marriage and sexuality in India.* Calcutta: Bhatkal and Sen.

Seth, V. (1993). *A suitable boy.* London: Phoenix House.

Sharda, B. D. (1990). Marriage markets and matrimonial match-making among Asian Indians of the United States. *International Journal of Sociology of the Family,* 20, 21–29.

Shaw, A. (1988). *A Pakistani community in Britain.* Oxford: Blackwell.

—— (2006). The arranged transnational cousin marriages of British Pakistanis: Critique, dissent and cultural continuity. *Contemporary South Asia,* 15(2), 209–220.

Shaw, A., and Charsley, K. (2006). Rishtas: Adding emotion to strategy in understanding British Pakistani transnational marriages. *Global Networks,* 6, 405–421.

Sheel, R. (2005). Marriage, money and gender: A case study of the migrant Indian community in Canada. *Indian Journal of Gender Studies,* 12(2–3), 335–356.

Shetty, S. (1995). (Dis)figuring the nation: Mother, metaphor, metonymy. *Differences: A Journal of Feminist Cultural Studies,* 7(3), 50–80.

Sidaway, J. (Ed.). (2002). *Postcolonial geographies: Survey-explore-review.* London: Continuum.

Silverman, D. (2000). *Doing qualitative research.* London: Sage.

Solomon, R. C. (1993). *The passions: Emotions and the meaning of life.* Indianapolis: Hackett.

Spivak, G. C. (1985). Three women's texts and a critique of imperialism. *Critical Inquiry,* 12(1), 243–249.

—— (1988). Can the subaltern speak? In C. Nelson and L. Grossberg (Eds.), *Marxism and the interpretation of culture.* Urbana: University of Illinois Press.

—— (1990). *The postcolonial critique: Interviews, strategies, dialogues.* New York: Routledge.

—— (1992). The politics of translation. In M. Barrett and A. Philips (Eds.), *Destabilising theory: Contemporary feminist debates.* Cambridge: Polity.

—— (1996). *The Spivak reader.* New York: Routledge.

—— (2003). *Death of a discipline.* New York: Columbia University Press.

Stopes-Roe, M., and Cochrane, R. (1990). *Citizens of this country: The Asian British.* Clevedon: Multilingual Matters.

Telang, S. (1967). *The coloured immigrant in Newcastle upon Tyne.* Newcastle upon Tyne: City Planning Department.

Temple, B., and Young, A. (2004). Qualitative research and translation dilemmas. *Qualitative Research,* 4(1), 161–179.

Thomas, R. (1996). Melodrama and the negotiation of morality in mainstream Hindi film. In C. Breckenridge (Ed.), *Consuming modernity: Public culture in contemporary India*. Delhi: Oxford University Press.

Titzmann, F. M. (2013). Changing patterns of matchmaking: The Indian online matrimonial market. *Asian Journal of Women's Studies*, 19, 64–94.

Tovar, P. (2001). Marriage. In C. Kramarae and D. Spender (Eds.), *Routledge international encyclopedia of women: Global women's issues and knowledge*. London: Routledge.

Twamley, K. (2014). *Love and marriage amongst Gujarati Indians in the UK and India: A suitable match*. Basingstoke: Palgrave Macmillan.

Tyler, I., and Marciniak, K. (2013). *Protesting citizenship: Migrant activisms*. Abingdon: Routledge.

Uberoi, P. (1998). The diaspora comes home: Disciplining desire in DDLJ. *Contributions to Indian Sociology*, 32(2), 305–336.

UK Border Agency. (2011). Family migration: A consultation. http://www.ukba.home office.gov.uk/sitecontent/documents/policyandlaw/consultations/family -migration/consultation.pdf?view=Binary.

Upreti, H. C. (1954). Matrimonial advertisements: A brief sociological analysis. *Journal of Family Welfare*, 14(1), 33–43.

Vertovec, S. (1994). Caught in the ethnic quandary: Indo-Caribbean Hindus. In R. Ballard (Ed.), *Desh Pardesh: The South Asian presence in Britain*. London: C. Hurst.

—— (2001). Transnational challenges to the "new" multiculturalism. Economic and Social Research Council Transnational Communities Programme Working Paper WPTC-01-06.

Vertovec, S., Clarke, C., and Peach, C. (1990). *South Asians overseas: Contexts and communities*. Cambridge: Cambridge University Press.

Walker, A., and Jolly, B. (2019). Dad made daughters who refused arranged marriage "feel like they were in prison." *Mirror*, June 18. https://www.mirror.co.uk/news /uk-news/dad-made-daughters-who-refused-16536211.

Wardlow, H. (2006). *Wayward women: Sexuality and agency in a New Guinea society*. Berkeley: University of California Press.

Weeks, J. (1995). *Invented moralities: Sexual values in an age of uncertainty*. New York: Columbia University Press.

Werbner, P. (1986). The virgin and the clown—Ritual elaboration in Pakistani migrants' weddings. *Man*, 21(2), 227–250.

—— (2007). Veiled interventions in pure space: Honour, shame and embodied struggles among Muslims in Britain and France. *Theory, Culture & Society*, 24(2), 161–186.

White, S. K. (2000). *Sustaining affirmation: The strengths of weak ontology in political theory*. Princeton, NJ: Princeton University Press.

Xiaohe, X., and Whyte, M. (1990). Love marriage and arranged marriages: A Chinese replication. *Journal of Marriage and the Family*, 31, 153–165.

Yeoh, B. S. A. (2013). "Upwards" or "sideways" cosmopolitanism? Talent/labour/marriage migrations in the globalising city-state of Singapore. *Migration Studies*, 1, 96–116.

Yuval-Davis, N. (2006). Human/women's rights and feminist transversal politics. In M. Ferree and A. Tripp (Eds.), *Transnational feminisms: Women's global activism and human rights*. New York: New York University Press.

Yuval-Davis, N., Wemyss, G., and Cassidy, K. (2018). Everyday bordering, belonging and the reorientation of British immigration legislation. *Sociology*, 52(2), 228–244.

INDEX

adoption, 75
advertisements, matrimonial, 36, 43, 44, 48–49, 50
agape, 79
Alok, 29–30, 91–93, 94
ambivalence, 9, 105
Amis, Martin, 1
Ancient Greece, 14, 79–80, 91
Anthias, Floya, 15, 16–17
apana, 37, 111
The Archaeology of Knowledge (Foucault), 35
arranged marriage practices, 112–118; arrangement process, 42–44; in Bollywood films, 5, 43, 56–57, 113; British immigration policy against, 1–3, 85, 112; defining, 6–8, 21–26; discourse of, 34–41; emotionality and intuition in, 55–56, 78, 82; family meeting rituals in, 28, 51–56; *vs.* forced marriage, 6, 25–26, 36–37, 39, 42, 59, 112; forced marriage as, 1, 4, 7–8, 98; media representation of, 1, 56; othering of, 1, 3–4, 8, 87, 112; research on, 8–15, 23–24, 96–98; ritualistic script for, 42–43, 56, 59–60; spectrum of, 26–34; spreading the word, 44–50; as term, 5, 25, 86. *See also* arranged weddings; love; love-cum-arranged marriages; modernity; semi-arranged marriages
arranged weddings, 5, 31–32, 34, 37, 116. *See also* arranged marriage practices
Ars Amatoria (Ovid), 80
Aslam, Mr., 107–111
Aunty Jis networks, 45–46
authenticity, 57

Baumann, Gerd, 38
beauty standards and marriage, 63–64, 73. *See also* "good girl"
belonging. *See* transnational belonging
Bhabha, Homi, 105
Bharatmatrimony.com, 49–50

BHP (biodata, horoscope, and photograph), 49
black-gori, 66–67
Bollywood films, 5, 43, 56–57, 113. *See also* media representations on arranged marriages
Brah, Avtar, 17
brides. *See* arranged marriage practices; "good girl"
Britain. *See* Great Britain
British Indian diaspora, overview, 12–17, 97. *See also* Indian culture; transnational belonging

capitalism, 81, 85, 86
caste and marriage preferences, 33, 48–50, 62–63, 88
character standards and marriage preferences, 54, 63, 66–68, 74–75
chinta, 44
church gatherings, 44, 47–48
citizenship: enactment of, 5, 13, 21, 40–41, 111, 116–117; immigration policies on arranged marriages and, 1–3, 85
class. *See* caste and marriage preferences
Cohen, Robin, 15–16
collective trauma, 16
colonialism, 10–11, 20, 98, 104–106. *See also* postcolonial frameworks
companionate love marriages. *See* love marriages
consanguineous marriage, as term, 6, 25, 26. *See also* arranged marriage practices
Coontz, Stephanie, 85
cricket, 9n1

Das, Sraboni, 29, 42
demotic discourse, 38–39. *See also* discourse of arranged marriage
Denmark, 3
diaspeirein, 14
diaspora, as term, 14, 17

diasporic communities, 14, 16–17. *See also* British Indian diaspora, overview
Dirlik, Arif, 10
discourse of arranged marriage, 34–41. *See also* arranged marriage practices
divorce, 46, 67, 100, 107. *See also* separation
dominant discourse, 38, 39. *See also* discourse of arranged marriage

economic migration, 13–14, 72, 84
educational background and marriage preferences, 49, 61–63, 64–65, 92
Ek acchhi ladki, 63
embodiment of cultural values, 68, 99–102. *See also* language considerations
emotionality, 55–56, 78, 82. *See also* love; romantic love
enacting citizenship, 40–41. *See also* citizenship
endogamous marriage, as term, 6. *See also* arranged marriage practices
Engels, Friedrich, 85–86
English. *See* language considerations
eros, 79
ethnic identity and marriage preferences, 30, 45, 62–63, 111. *See also* British Indian diaspora, overview; Indian culture
ethnographic fieldwork, 13–14

family meetings, 28, 51–56, 59–60. *See also* arranged marriage practices; kinship considerations *vs.* individual choice; parental consent
femininity. *See* "good girl"
feminist theory on gender and relationships, 23, 68, 73, 78, 81–83
film industry. *See* Bollywood films
first-generation, as term, 13
forced marriages: *vs.* arranged marriages, 6, 25–26, 36–37, 39, 42, 59, 112; arranged marriages as, 1, 4, 7–8, 98; illegality of, 87
Foucault, Michel, 10, 35

The Gay Science (Nietzsche), 93
gender roles: in arranged family meetings, 52–53; "good girl," xiv, 51, 53, 63–76, 113, 117; "suitable boy," xiv, 60–63, 68, 71–72, 74, 76, 113, 117; "traditional-minded modern girl," 20, 65–66, 68, 74
genealogy of love, 79–83. *See also* love
Ghalib, 90
Gilroy, Paul, 14, 110
glasses, 73–74
Global Diasporas (Cohen), 15–16
"good citizen" policies, 2–3

"good girl," xiv, 51, 53, 63–76, 113, 117. *See also* gender roles; "traditional-minded modern girl"
gori, 66–67
Gosh, Amitav, 16
Great Britain: British Indian diaspora in, overview, 14–17, 97; immigration policies of, 1–3, 85, 112; research site of, 13–14
Greek tradition and love, 14, 79–80, 91
grooms. *See* arranged marriage practices; "suitable boy"
gurudwara gatherings, 44, 47–48, 50

Hindi. *See* language considerations
Hindu populations, 14, 44, 47–48, 50, 56–57, 91, 102
Hindustan Times (HT), 48
horoscope, 49

identity, 12–13. *See also* British Indian diaspora, overview; Indian culture; othering; transnational belonging
Immigration and Asylum Act (2002), 2
immigration policies, 1–3, 85, 112
Indian culture: British Indian diaspora, overview, 12–17, 97; embodiment of, 68, 99–102; gatherings and match-making process in, 44, 47–48, 50; Hindu population, 14, 56–57, 91, 102; language and, 18–20, 87–88; Mr. Pandara on, 104; Muslim population, 6, 14, 26, 107–111; Sikh population, 14, 102–107. *See also* British Indian diaspora, overview; transnational belonging
individual choice *vs.* kinship considerations, 1, 4–5, 33, 92–93, 97. *See also* parental consent
Industrialism, 85. *See also* modernity
intimacy, politics of, 82, 84–87. *See also* love
intuition, 55–56

Jagger, Alison, 78–79
ji. See Aunty Jis networks
jobs: marriage preference and, 49, 61–63, 65, 71–72, 92, 100; migration and, 13–14, 72, 84

Kanta, 29–30, 91–93, 94
kinship considerations *vs.* individual choice, 1, 4–5, 92–93, 97. *See also* parental consent
kinship studies, 97
Kumaoni. *See* language considerations

ladka dekhna / ladki dekhna, 60
language considerations, 18–20, 87–88. *See also* embodiment of cultural values

Leach, Edmund, 1
Leonard, Diana, 82
liberalism, 85, 86, 100–101
love: in a British Indian context, 93–95;
    history of romantic love, 27–29, 79–83,
    113–114; politics of intimacy in, 82,
    84–87; as social construct, 78–79,
    88–89; stories of, 89–93, 95; as term,
    86, 87–88. See also emotionality; love
    marriages
love-cum-arranged marriages: descrip-
    tion of, 5, 20, 27, 29–30, 32; example
    of, 91–92; as modern, 36, 37, 113.
    See also arranged marriage practices
"Love Laws," 88
love marriages, 1, 70, 77, 85–87, 95.
    See also love; love-cum-arranged
    marriages
ludus, 79

mail-order brides, 7, 23, 84
mania, 79
marriage, defined, 21–22. See also
    arranged marriage practices
marriage preferences: beauty standards
    in, 63–64, 73; caste, 33, 48–50, 62–63,
    88; character standards, 54, 63, 66–68,
    74–75; educational and professional
    background, 49, 61–63, 64–65, 71–72,
    92, 100; ethnic identity, 30, 45, 62–63,
    111. See also "good girl"; "suitable boy"
marriage-related migration, 1–4, 72,
    84–85, 111
masculinity. See "suitable boy"
matchmaking, 6, 26–28, 44, 46–47.
    See also arranged marriage practices
matrimonial advertisements and
    websites, 48–50
media representations on arranged
    marriages, 1, 56. See also Bollywood
    films
men. See "suitable boy"
migration: of 1990s, 13–14; culturally-
    defined terms on, 12; economic, 13–14,
    72, 84; marriage-related, 1–4, 72,
    84–85, 111
"Of Mimicry and Man" (Bhabha), 105
modernity: aspects of arranged marriage
    as, 5, 30–31, 94, 103, 113, 115–116, 118;
    discourse on arranged marriage as, 21,
    36–38, 44; enacting citizenship as,
    40–41, 116–117; "good girl" character
    and, 24, 65–67; love-based marriage
    as, 85–87, 95; romantic love and, 5,
    80–82. See also arranged marriage
    practices
Mohammad, Robina, 24–25
multicultural conviviality, 110
Muslim populations, 6, 14, 26, 107–111

neoliberalism, 85, 86
Netherlands, 3
newspaper advertisements, 36, 43, 44,
    48–49, 50
Nietzsche, Friedrich, 93
nonresident (NRI) Indian marriages, 5,
    43, 49, 57
Norway, 3

The Origins of the Family, Private Property
    and the State (Engels), 85–86
othering, 1, 3–4, 8, 87, 97, 112. See also
    identity; transnational belonging
Oxford English Dictionary, 23, 80

Pakistani women, 24
Pal, Mr. and Mrs., 89–91, 94
Pandara, Mr., 102–107
paraya, 37, 111
parental consent, 29–32, 33. See also
    family meetings; kinship consider-
    ations vs. individual choice
performance: of citizenship, 5, 13, 21,
    40–41, 111, 116–117; exercises in
    arranged marriage, 36–37; ritual of
    family meetings, 28, 52–56
Persian poetry, 90n2
philia, 79
photograph, 49
poetry, 88, 90n2
political economy of marriage, 72–73.
    See also professional qualifications and
    marriage preferences
politics of intimacy, 82, 84–87
pooch taach, 55
postcolonial frameworks, 9–13. See also
    colonialism; modernity
pragma, 79
pregnancy, 75
professional qualifications and marriage
    preferences, 49, 61–63, 65, 71–72, 92,
    100
Punjabi. See language considerations
pyar, 87. See also love

racialized immigration policies, 1–3
reason-emotion dualism, 55–56, 78–79.
    See also emotionality
research, overview, 8–15, 23–24, 96–98
rishta, 20, 46, 64
romantic love, 27–29, 79–83, 113–114. See
    also love
Romantic movement, 80, 85
Routledge International Encyclopedia of
    Women, 22
Roy, Arundhati, 88

Saint Augustine, 79
second-generation, as term, 13

"Secure Borders, Safe Haven: Integration with Diversity in Modern Britain" (2001), 2
Select Committee on Race Relations and Immigration (1976), 2
semi-arranged marriages: description of, 5, 27, 32, 71; as modern, 33, 36, 37, 39, 113; of second-generation migrants, 28–29. *See also* arranged marriage practices
separation, 93. *See also* divorce
Seth, Vikram, 61
sexlove, 85
Shaadi.com, 49
shaadi mela, 48
Sharma, Shusheela, 63–64, 98–102, 107, 111
Sikh population, 14, 44, 47–48, 50, 102–107
single parenting, 100
Socrates, 79
spectrum of arranged marriages, 26–34. *See also* arranged marriage practices
spousal leave policy, 2
"spreading the word," in arranged marriage process, 44–50. *See also* arranged marriage practices
standards of beauty, 63–64, 73. *See also* "good girl"
storge, 79, 91
strategic essentialism, 105

"suitable boy," xiv, 60–63, 68, 71–72, 74, 76, 113, 117. *See also* gender roles

temple gatherings, 44, 47–48, 50
third-generation, as term, 12
Times of India (publication), 48
traditional arranged marriages. *See* arranged marriage practices; forced marriages
"traditional-minded modern girl," 20, 65–66, 68, 74. *See also* "good girl"
translation. *See* language considerations
transnational belonging, 1–3, 16–17, 59–60. *See also* British Indian diaspora, overview; Indian culture
transnational marriage, as term, 7, 25, 26. *See also* arranged marriage practices

Ugandan Asians, 16
Urdu. *See* language considerations
Urdu poetry, 88, 90n2

websites, 49–50
Weeks, James, 68–69
Western notions of love and marriage, 1, 79–81, 95, 100–101
whiteness, 66–67
women. *See* "good girl"; "traditional-minded modern girl"
work. *See* jobs
worlding, 11–12